Finalist, Dartmouth Book Award for Non-Fiction

Finalist, Taste Canada Awards (Culinary Narratives)

Nominee, three Gourmand Awards (Food Culture)

A *Hill Times* Top 100 Selection

An Atlantic Bestseller

"Remarkable." — *East Coast Living*

"Inspiring, uplifting, and essential reading for all."
—James Mullinger, [EDIT]

"I admit that when reading this, I had a few tears and
felt so proud to be a Canadian!" — *Canadian Cookbooks*

"Sad and sometimes harrowing, it is testament to the strength
a loving family possesses, giving its members the endurance
to overcome seemingly impossible odds." — *Oakville News*

"A story that reminds us that even against enormous odds
positive outcomes are possible and that remarkable things
can be accomplished through hard work and perseverance."
— *Miramichi Reader*

"*Peace by Chocolate* tells the story of one family, but it also tells
the story of people in Antigonish, who like so many welcoming
communities across Canada, sponsored Syrian refugees, and helped
them settle into an unfamiliar country." — *Chronicle Herald*

JON TATTRIE

Peace by

The Hadhad Family's
Remarkable Journey
from Syria to Canada

Chocolate

GOOSE LANE

Edited by Jill Ainsley.
Cover and page design by Julie Scriver.
Cover photography by James Smeaton, jamesphotos.ca.
Printed in Canada by Rapido Books.
20 19 18 17 16

Library and Archives Canada Cataloguing in Publication

Title: Peace by Chocolate : the Hadhad family's remarkable journey
from Syria to Canada / Jon Tattrie.
Names: Tattrie, Jon, author.
Identifiers: Canadiana (print) 20200216279 | Canadiana (ebook) 20200216287 | ISBN
9781773101897 (softcover) | ISBN 9781773101903 (EPUB) | ISBN 9781773101910 (Kindle)
Subjects: LCSH: Hadhad, Isam—Family. | LCSH: Peace by Chocolate (Firm)—Biography. |
LCSH: Peace by Chocolate (Firm)—History. | LCSH: Syrians—Nova Scotia—
Antigonish—Biography. | CSH: Syrian Canadians—Nova Scotia—Antigonish—Biography |
LCSH: Refugees—Nova Scotia—Antigonish—Biography. | LCSH: Refugees—Syria—
Biography. | LCSH: Confectioners—Nova Scotia—Antigonish—Biography. |
LCSH: Chocolate industry—Nova Scotia—Antigonish—History. |
LCSH: Antigonish (N.S.)—Biography. | LCGFT: Biographies.
Classification: LCC FC2349.A58 Z7 2020 | DDC 971.6/14—dc23

Goose Lane Editions acknowledges the generous support of the Government of Canada,
the Canada Council for the Arts, and the Government of New Brunswick.

Goose Lane Editions is located on the unceded territory of the Wəlastəkwiyik whose
ancestors along with the Mi'kmaq and Peskotomuhkati Nations signed Peace and
Friendship Treaties with the British Crown in the 1700s.

Goose Lane Editions
500 Beaverbrook Court, Suite 330
Fredericton, New Brunswick
CANADA E3B 5X4
gooselane.com

Nova Scotia strong.

Contents

Prologue

Theobroma cacao is a strange tree. Its slender green leaves drip with water in the humid Amazon rainforest it calls home. It loves moisture. If it gets shade from the sun, and protection from the wind, it can grow as high as ten metres. Some trees grow alone, while others flourish in families. White and pink star-shaped flowers sprout directly from the trunk. When pollinated, they produce a fruit known as a cacao pod. The red or yellow pods grow about thirty centimetres long and ten centimetres wide. Their skin is almost as hard as a coconut shell.

Monkeys, squirrels, rats, and bats were the first creatures to learn the secrets of the chocolate tree, but the gods weren't far behind. The animals gnawed open the pods, which never drop from their trees, and harvested the sweet milky pulp inside, tossing aside the brown seeds or beans.

Eventually, people living in the eastern foothills of the Andes observed the animals devouring the cacao pods and tried the pulp themselves. One day, thousands of years ago, a forgotten genius decided to collect the beans from the pulp and roast them. "Cacao seeds were mashed to make a crude, bitter-tasting paste, [and] mixed with water, chile peppers, vanilla, and other spices and maize to prepare a revered beverage," zoologist Allen M. Young notes. The taste changed the way the ancient people looked at the tree, a change reflected in the name it was later given: *Theobroma cacao*, the food of the gods. "To prehistoric Mesoamericans," writes Young, "the cacao tree was the embodiment of the Earth's treasures and spiritually represented a bridge between Earth and the heavens."

People used the pods as money as far back at 1600 BCE, or as a sacrifice to the gods in return for rain and healthy crops. The devout put chocolate beans at the centre of mystical rites. The fat pods were stowed in canoes and transported great distances, where they held high value for those who had no access to the chocolate tree. The fruit of the tree spread to the Olmec people of the Gulf Coast of Mexico. The Mayans used chocolate drinks and included images of chocolate trees and cacao pods in their sculptures of warrior priests and nobility. At the ancient city of Chichen Iza, a Mayan lord clutches a chocolate tree with a strong right arm. Cacao pods decorated stone incense burners. Regular people spent chocolate coins, and when the coin was too old to be accepted as money, they melted it into a drink for a sacred sendoff. The Mayan ruler of Tikal in modern Guatemala took on the name Lord Cacao 1,300 years ago to show his wealth. The Mayan dead took chocolate drinks to the grave for sustenance in the afterlife.

The Aztecs forced conquered people to pay tribute in cacao beans and amassed great wealth. In Tenochtitlan, their capital in the Valley of Mexico, warehouses filled with cacao beans. Proto-chocolatiers sun-dried the beans then roasted them and ground them into a paste mixed with water. They added vanilla or maize, patted it into a little cake, and stored it for later use. When the rulers called for chocolate drink, the chocolatiers broke off a piece of the cake and added water and red achiote. It poured out like blood as they tumbled it between vessels to make a frothy drink. Finally, they poured it into a crafted tortoise shell and handed it to the ruler. They called it chocolatl.

The great Montezuma built several large warehouses to store his cacao cakes and protected his wealth like it was gold or silver.

When marauding Europeans overran the ancient world five hundred years ago, the conquering Spanish quickly developed a taste for it. Under Spanish rule, a rabbit cost ten beans, a horse fifty, a slave one hundred. Prostitutes charged the conquistadors ten cacao beans. The brutal Hernando Cortés once said, "He who has drunk one cup can travel a whole day without any further food."

Orchards expanded, and a rich farmer could grow thirty-three thousand chocolate trees, producing four hundred thousand cacao beans a year. The first chocolate patties reached Europe in 1530. Cooks mixed sugar and cinnamon into the paste. Nuts, powdered white roses, and orange water added flavour. For the next hundred years, until tea and coffee arrived, chocolate was the sole source of liquid caffeine. At a time when water was often too dirty to drink, chocolate was a safe, popular beverage.

Europeans forced African and Indigenous slaves to harvest sugar cane in the Caribbean to sweeten the chocolate. European monks, soldiers, and travellers swore by the restorative drink. Some claimed it was a medicine that healed your heart; others said it stirred lust in the loins. For lovers, it was an expensive gift. The English mixed milk into the chocolate, giving it a smoother texture, and companies invested heavily to bring the chocolate drink to regular people. By 1820, the English consumed five hundred tons a year. Half was said to go into the bellies of the navy, often mixed as chocolate rum.

In the United States, Thomas Jefferson boasted that "the superiority of chocolate, both for health and nourishment, would soon give it the same preference over tea that it has in Spain." In 1828, Coenraad van Houten turned the cacao into a powder, not a paste, and invented a mechanical press that removed the fat from the beans. The powder was mixed with cacao butter and sugar in 1848 to create the first chocolate designed to be eaten, not drunk. In 1875, the Swiss created solid milk chocolate. Soon, chocolate bars and chocolate candies put the food of the gods in the hands of all mortals. Chocolatiers perfected the treat's trademark melt-in-your-mouth sensation.

By the twenty-first century, people all around the world were consuming 3.4 million cacao beans each year. Well-funded attempts to make chocolate in the laboratory have failed. Every piece of chocolate in the world still traces its roots to the sacred chocolate tree. Even today, the vast majority of cacao, 80 per cent, grows in small farms in humid rainforests. Twice a year, workers machete the pods off the trees, crack them open, and remove the beans. The farmers ferment the beans and spread them out to dry under the sun. Soon, a pleasant chocolate scent wafts through the air. The beans are cleaned and roasted in ovens before workers crack them open and grind the inner nibs into a chocolate liquor, which is pressed into a small tablet. The liquor is sold to chocolate makers and turned into all manner of chocolate treats, which take their place in shops, restaurants, and homes around the world.

Many people know how to make raw chocolate, but no one understands why the process works. The ritual remains steeped in mystery. The five hundred chemicals modern scientists have found in chocolate brew up an intoxicating mix. It's scientific proof of what chocolate lovers have always known to be true: chocolate makes happiness.

Part One

One

Isam Hadhad first fell in love with chocolate as a child. He lived with his mother, father, sisters, and brothers in the ancient city of Damascus, a green oasis in a lifeless desert. Some traditions say Damascus is where God breathed life into dust, created humans in God's own image, and blessed them, and that deep under Damascus lie the ruined walls of the Garden of Eden. Adam and Eve climbed the slopes of Mount Qasioun and prayed in its caves. They celebrated the birth of their first son, Cain, and their second-born, Abel, in the mountain's shadow. (In Islam, Cain and Abel are known as Qabil and Habil.) But Cain turned on Abel and smashed his head in with a rock. The Qur'an tells us if you murder one of your brothers or sisters, you have murdered all humanity; if you save one life, you have saved all humanity.

Archaeological evidence proves the oasis was inhabited six thousand years ago. Under today's Old City, scientists have found pottery from five thousand years ago. The name first appeared in print in Egypt, when in 1490 BCE scribes recorded that Thutmose III had conquered Damascus.

In 1516, Turkish forces won the land and brought it into the Ottoman Empire for four centuries. Mark Twain visited in 1867 and ascended to the top of Mount Qasioun on horseback. The ancient city lay at his feet. "As the glare of day mellowed into twilight, we looked down upon a picture which is celebrated all over the world," he wrote. "Go back as far as you will into the vague past: there was always a Damascus. In the writings of every century for more than four thousand years, its name has been mentioned and its praises sung. To Damascus, years are only moments, decades are only flitting trifles of time. She measures time not by days and months and years, but by the empires she has seen rise, and prosper, and crumble to ruin."

During World War I, Arab troops captured Syria and ended Ottoman rule. In 1919, Syria held elections, and Faysal I was crowned king of Syria. France attacked and made Syria a French mandate. France drew a new borderline, parting Lebanon from Syria. Syrian rebels fought French rule; France bombed Damascus in the 1920s. Syria won its independence from France in 1936, but France, worried about Hitler and the implications of losing its Middle East territories, deferred ratification of the treaty. France attacked Damascus again after the war, killing hundreds of people, before withdrawing from Syria for good in 1946. In the years that followed, Syria endured coups, countercoups, and foreign meddling until 1963, when the Ba'ath Party took control.

The Hadhad family home was a wide, rectangular structure made primarily of concrete. It was located in the al-Midan suburb, just south of the Old City's walls and close to the modern centre. The neighbourhood's crowded, narrow streets and alleys are famed for the many scholars born there and for the traditional sweet shops selling pastries such as baklava and sweet cheese rolls. When Isam's grandfather started to build the house decades earlier, he laid a deep foundation but built only one storey. He dreamed that the air above it would one day be filled with new storeys for his children and their children. In the 1970s, Isam's parents added another storey, a self-contained home, and connected it to the first by an exterior staircase. They added a third storey in the early 1980s. Isam, his parents, his three brothers, and his three sisters lived on the ground floor. Above them lived three of his uncles, their wives, and their children. About twenty-five relatives lived in the building by the time Isam entered his teenage years. The sprawling Hadhad clan gathered at that time to discuss an idea: should they build even higher on the foundation their ancestor had laid? After many late-night cups of tea, they answered yes. In an extended growth spurt, the Damascus house acquired a fourth, fifth, sixth, seventh, eighth, ninth, and finally tenth floor. The top floor offered breathtaking views of nearby Andalus Park and the ancient city's southern district. On clear days, you could glimpse Mount Qasioun.

Modern Damascus is a sprawling city, home to 2.7 million people, but Isam and his six siblings grew up in a spacious, green community, playing soccer on the streets and running through the fields, until new houses sprouted in the empty spaces and the neighbourhood became indistinguishable from the rest of the capital. Even as the dust and noise of the city surrounded it, when you were on Hadhad land, you felt you were in an oasis of peace and quiet. A small indoor courtyard with a water fountain hosted most of the festivities. In one corner, an open-air *iwan* had a second fountain where everyone gathered in the summer. A swing hung nearby, and children loved to pump their legs to see if they could turn a full circle. In the garden grew apricots, olives, figs, Damascus berries, and a pretty white flower called Damascene jasmine. The top of the apricot tree that once nodded against a first-storey window grew until it bent into a bedroom window on the second storey.

On special occasions, hundreds of people would celebrate at the Hadhad home. Isam loved Eid-al-Fitr, the feast to celebrate the end of Ramadan, the month of fasting. Family would come from all across Syria to the Damascus house. First came prayers, thanks to God for life and its blessings. Then came feasting, music, and dancing. When there was a family wedding, the bachelor's celebration happened at their home. The groom would arrive with all his male relatives. Music would play as the men danced. Any neighbours who heard the commotion would hurry over to join the party. As a boy, Isam wasn't always clear on who were near neighbours and who were family. It seemed like the same thing.

Like all Syrian men, Isam was required to serve in the military for three years. He deferred his service until after he'd completed his engineering degree. He was twenty when he began his service; most of the other new recruits were still teenagers. Some of these boys looked to him almost as a father figure, which he liked. When it came time to parachute out of a plane during training, Isam jumped first to reassure the others. The fourth time he jumped, he almost enjoyed it.

Isam completed his military service at a time of relative peace in the Middle East. When he was four, Syria's armed forces had gone to war with Israel in the Six-Day War, losing the Golan Heights. In 1970, when he was seven, Syrian forces got tangled up in a conflict between Jordan, Palestine, and Israel. Unrest led the minister of defence, Hafez al-Assad, to launch a bloodless coup and seize power that year. Three years after that, Syria tried and failed to take back the Golan Heights; in the years that followed, an uneasy truce had held between Syria and Israel. The civil war next door in Lebanon terrified Syrians, but by 1986 it seemed to be stabilizing. Isam's three years in uniform in the mid-1980s had passed mostly uneventfully. He felt on the brink of a time of peace and prosperity in his nation and his own life. Even the United Nations had declared 1986 the International Year of Peace.

Tasting chocolate imported from Europe for a cousin's wedding changed Isam's life. He was at the *talbeeseh*, the groom's celebration, with all his male relatives. Isam slipped a chocolate into his mouth and smiled as the smooth exterior melted on his tongue and slid down his throat. Isam was transfixed. He didn't know a single person who made chocolate. He had no clue how he could win a wife and support a family by making chocolate. But it was clear nonetheless: he needed to make chocolate.

Isam raced home from his cousin's wedding to his mother's kitchen. He stood still for a few moments. This was not a familiar room. It took him a while to assemble the pots and pans he thought he would need. He found a recipe for chocolate and tried to follow the instructions carefully. He failed and produced a brown puddle. He borrowed books that claimed to hold the secret to the perfect batch. He failed again. He thought his frustration made the chocolates bitter, so he willed himself into a state of calm.

Chocolate fascinated him. He loved how you could make a tiny piece that balanced on your finger, or enough to fill a factory. He realized he was an artist, and chocolate was his medium. It was intimate, edible art. He loved it in its melted stage, a warm liquid that could be poured to take the shape of any mould: a flower, an animal, a heart, a star, or an intricate pattern. Once in the mould, it hardened. *Just like people*, he thought. *We are born with our raw ingredients, heated and stirred by our early lives, and poured out into a mould called adulthood. But the chocolate is not the mould, and neither are people. You can always melt chocolate and make it into a new shape.*

He also grew obsessed with the ancient ritual of making chocolate. Any time he ate in a restaurant, he listened patiently through the dessert options until they mentioned their finest chocolate. He consumed it, studying the texture and taste, how smoothly it melted, what sweet aftertaste remained. He turned his nose up at chocolate-covered candy. Only premium chocolate would do. Pure, dark, and deep, every bite releasing happiness.

He gained control over the mysterious process. He melted the raw cocoa, sweetened it with sugar, added nuts and dried fruits, and poured it into moulds. His family and friends felt their mouths watering as he approached, bringing the scent of chocolate with him. He put down the recipes and followed his heart. The happier he was, the sweeter the chocolate. He took boxes of chocolate on the bus and visited gift shops. He gave the owners free samples and promised to return. If the gifted chocolate sold, perhaps they would be interested in buying some?

Everyone loved his chocolate, except for his mother. Well, she loved the chocolate, but not the mess in her kitchen. Isam would whip up a batch and then abandon the mess of pots and pans. His mother scrubbed the brown splatter off her cupboards and counters several times before she complained. He promised to find his own kitchen. But he still couldn't find the nerve to tell her he planned to make chocolate his life's work.

In the summer of 1986, Isam and his closest friends took a six-hour bus ride from Damascus to Latakia, Syria, to spend a week at the beach. They played beach volleyball and swam in the ocean. In the evening, Isam sought some time to himself to come to grips with the big decision he was about to make. On the last night, he walked along the beach, feeling the damp sand crumble between his toes. The Mediterranean Sea tried to climb up the beach, then sighed, fell away, and tried again. Children chased it out and fled in gales of laughter when it returned.

He savoured the sunset. His breathing slowed as the sun melted into the sea. He'd always been drawn to the water. Damascus was so dry. Like many Syrians, he felt a constant thirst that led him to lakes, rivers, and the open sea.

The waves deepened his meditation. Happiness rose in his heart as the sun slipped away in a red blaze, but anxiety churned in his stomach. He knew what he wanted could upset his family and jeopardize his future. His mother had long hoped he would grow up to be a doctor or an engineer. He'd picked engineering, and his family expected he would start a stable career. It would allow him to marry, have children, and provide a good life for them.

His father had devoted his professional life to the government, working in the legal department for long hours and providing his family with a comfortable middle-class life. His father's closest friends had all grown up and had sons and daughters; those sons were Isam's closest friends. Isam was expected to make the same choices. But he knew he had to follow his dream, or he'd regret it forever. Now, as he walked along the sandy beach, he decided it was time for courage.

Once home, he sat down with his mother and father.

"I don't want to be a civil engineer," he told them.

"Well, what are you going to be?" his mother asked him.

"I'm going to make chocolate."

The news took a moment to sink in. "Why?" she asked.

. He took a moment to answer. "I want to have an impact on the community I live in, and being a civil engineer isn't my passion anymore."

His parents were stunned. It seemed to them that a civil engineer was more likely to have an impact on his community than a chocolate maker. Life in Syria could be unstable at the best of times, as governments rose and fell and peace ebbed and flowed. Why would he throw away his education and prospects to make sweets? They made it clear that they would not support his choice, but they also said that they would not stand in his way.

He rented a small shop on the road to the Damascus airport. He turned the back into a tiny, one-person chocolate factory and created a gift shop in the front. His family watched uneasily. It was one thing for a man to make chocolate for fun. Could it really build a career? But Isam had a romantic notion of following his chocolate dream to achieve independence. He had a strange certainty that chocolate would provide for his family, should he be blessed with a wife and children. After he'd been in business for a full year, his family finally saw his passion and the success he was already enjoying, and they threw their support behind him.

Isam's shop, Hadhad Chocolate, flourished. People travelling to the airport often stopped in to buy a box of chocolates to take on their journey. When they stepped inside and smelled the freshly made chocolate, the sale was already nearly complete. He saved his profits to expand his business. He would build a strong foundation and rise, just as his grandfather had done when he built the family home. On Valentine's Day in 1987, Isam was melting raw chocolate in the tiny factory in the back when the shop door opened.

He looked up, ready to launch into the charming chatter that won him loyal customers, but fell silent. A beautiful young woman was standing in his store, looking at his chocolates. He watched her move hesitantly. He knew she'd leave soon.

"Hello," he forced himself to say. "My name is Isam. What's your name?"

She smiled. "My name is Shahnaz."

"Shahnaz," he said, enjoying the sound. "What can I get for you today?"

The young woman told him her family had gone to Istanbul, Turkey, for a short visit. She was supposed to join them, but she'd just missed her flight. It would have been the first time she'd been on a plane and the first time she'd left Syria. But now she was heading home and wanted to buy chocolates as a gift to welcome her family home in a few days. Which box would he recommend?

Isam said he would mix the perfect box for her. As they talked, he assembled two boxes of premium chocolates mixed with hazelnuts, crushed coconut, and dried fruits. It was a business trick, of course: when he carefully packed each box by hand, customers felt special. They ate the chocolates as slowly as he packed them. But on this day, he packed the chocolates slowly because he did not want Shahnaz to leave.

"One moment," he told her. He stepped into the tiny factory at the back of the building. He found a clean piece of paper and wrote on it. He returned to the shop and added a last chocolate to the boxes. He slipped the paper in without her noticing and handed her the chocolates. He refused to take her money.

"*Shukraan*," she said. Thank you.

Isam and Shahnaz smiled at each other.

Later, when she opened the box, the piece of paper fell out. She unfolded it. "I do not make chocolate," Isam had written. "I make happiness."

Her heart melted. She found a reason to return to the chocolate shop and the soft-centred man with the sweet exterior, and two years later they married.

After their wedding, Isam and Shahnaz moved into the second storey of the Hadhad's Damascus home. She chose the room with the apricot tree in the window as their bedroom. Through her window, she saw good things—lemon, orange, and apple trees. Cats roamed through the yard, and bats flittered in the night sky. She saw people, too, walking down the streets and sidewalks. This was a friendly neighbourhood.

They thanked Allah for blessing them with a daughter, whom they named Kenana. Another girl, Alaa, followed. In 1992, Shahnaz gave birth to their first son, and they named him Tareq.

Isam's business grew, too. In 1995, he left the little gift shop on the airport road and moved into a one-floor factory in Damascus's eastern industrial district. His religion forbade him from borrowing money with interest, so he earned and saved until he had enough to equip his new chocolate factory. He hired two people. He planned to build a second floor on the factory, and perhaps even a third.

At first, he used pots and pans to heat, melt, and mix the raw chocolate with the rest of his recipe. It tasted good, but the process was too inconsistent to scale up. He needed better tools. At great expense, he imported high-end European machines. He hired more people. They made more chocolate. Inspired by his trips to the beach at Latakia, he created a seashell-shaped line of chocolates that sold well. The Hadhad name started to become known in Damascus.

Shahnaz encouraged him to use his social gifts to grow the business. He had a knack for making friends: at school, in the military, at the judo classes he attended for three years (he earned a blue belt). Isam's ten best friends recommended him to their friends and family, and they in turn connected him to their networks. Soon he had contacts across Syria. He relied on friends and a close inner circle of trusted associates to turn a few pieces of chocolate given away into a flourishing business.

In 2000, he spent thousands of dollars on a new Nokia 3310 cellular phone. He was among the first Syrians to get a mobile phone, and it became his constant companion. While he was out, he'd slide it out of his pocket, scroll through his contacts, and press the green phone button to place the call. He loved letting them hear the street sounds and slowly realize he wasn't on a landline: he was on a cellphone. The sight of Isam pressing the stout plastic rectangle to his ear, convincing another buyer to try Hadhad Chocolate, became iconic around his factory in the industrial district. He now ran the second-biggest chocolate company in the Middle East.

Isam built giving into the foundation of Hadhad Chocolate. As he profited from his work, so would others. Giving is a fundamental part of traditional Syrian culture and one of Islam's Five Pillars. *Zakat*, or almsgiving, reminds people that everything belongs to God and individuals should feel no pride in passing God's gifts to those in greater need. As you give in times of plenty, so God will give to you in times of need. *Zakat* should be distributed in the community from which it was earned. He gathered his family around the table in the evenings to consider requests to help pay for medical treatment or to provide for orphans. He learned of some of these requests through Tareq, who would talk to people on the street and learn that they had lost their homes or family members, or that they had been hurt in a car accident or at work. Isam wanted his children to know the importance of sharing their success; they could one day be the people in need. The Hadhads always sent the money through an intermediary so that the recipients never knew the source of the gift.

But in June 2000, Syria plunged into a period of official mourning when, after thirty years in power, President Hafez al-Assad died. Radio and television stations stopped regular programming and instead read from the Qur'an and spoke about the late leader. Shops, schools, and public offices closed. Hotels stopped selling alcohol as a mark of respect. The *New York Times* said he'd transformed Syria from "a Middle East backwater into an introverted regional power." He had ended decades of coups and wars and poured money into building roads, schools, and hospitals. In public, he and his family wore plain clothes and looked like ordinary people. He ruled with ancient brutality. In 1982, he had thousands of people killed in Hama to stop an Islamic insurgency. He ran a police state and didn't trust anyone. He barred fax machines lest people somehow use them to overthrow the government. In 1980, rebels threw grenades at al-Assad. The president kicked one away, and his bodyguard jumped on the other one, sacrificing his life to save al-Assad. In the end, he died of a heart attack at sixty-nine.

Syrians were naturally anxious. According to the Syrian constitution, only people aged forty or older could be president. Al-Assad's heir apparent, his son Bashar, was only thirty-four. The constitution was quickly amended to lower the minimum age, and Bashar al-Assad ran unopposed. He claimed more than 97 per cent of the vote.

Bashar al-Assad appeared a reluctant ruler. He had graduated from the medical school of Damascus University in 1988—the year

Isam and Shahnaz were married—and started a career as an eye doctor. He seemed content to live a quiet, private life and leave politics to his older brother Bassel. Bassel had been destined to rule since birth, and every Syrian knew his face. He ran a brigade in the Republican Guard, and the media called him the Golden Knight. Bassel knew people feared him, so he disarmed them with jokes. He studied political systems around the world. He told people that he wanted to build a united country where no one was judged by their ethnicity or gender, to follow his father's work in creating a Syria free from sectarian troubles, where people were not defined as Sunni or Shia or Alawite—the al-Assads' clan—but as Syrians. It was not to be. On a foggy January day in 1994, Bassel sped past Isam's chocolate shop on the way to the Damascus airport. He lost control, hit a barrier, and flipped his car. The crash killed him and changed his younger brother's career path.

When Bashar al-Assad became president in 2000, a wave of hope lifted Syria. The eye doctor presented himself as an open-minded, cultured man who had studied in the West. Intelligent Syrians gathered in *muntadayats*, or salons, to talk about how politics could improve life in the ancient country. Members of suppressed groups started to speak openly. People called it the Damascus Spring. They urged the new government to release political prisoners, to end martial law, and to give its citizens free speech. Al-Assad did free hundreds of political opponents. But in 2001, he crushed the Damascus Spring. It seemed he had borrowed a trick from the Chinese dictator Mao Zedong and let "one hundred flowers blossom," luring his enemies out of their hiding places only to cut them down.

It was a sombre, secret principle in Syria: so long as no one talked about politics, or got involved in politics, or knew anyone involved in politics, life could be good. It was a principle Isam Hadhad followed. He wasn't interested in political activism. He just wanted to make chocolate, and in the first few years of the new regime, that seemed possible. Between 2005 and 2008, Syria opened to the world, and Isam often gave European clients tours of his factory. They loved the product and were drawn to the story's roots. Swedes and Germans, in particular, developed a taste for Syrian chocolate. When they came to Syria, their tour guides called Isam on his cellphone. Street signs were rare, so he would direct them to the transit stops and the pharmacy that signposted his factory. Android phones dominated the Syrian market, and Isam favoured the Samsung line. By the late 2000s, he was using a Samsung Instinct. He always upgraded to the newest phone.

Isam disliked leaving Damascus, let alone Syria, and avoided travelling for work. He had little formal training in business and worked the old-fashioned way: great product, word of mouth, and trust. He had advisers and product development teams, of course, but new chocolate products went through the family first. "What do you think?" he would ask. "Do you think it really fits into our excellence? Should we do anything else?"

By 2010, Kenana and Alaa had married and lived nearby with their husbands. Tareq was a young man with little interest in his father's business. He had his heart set on becoming a doctor and spent most of his days learning at Damascus University's medical school, studying at home, or meeting his friends to go over material. Since Tareq's birth in 1992, three more girls and a boy had blessed Isam and Shahnaz: Walaa, a wise girl on the cusp of womanhood; Batoul, a teenager; their second son, Ahmad; and his younger sister, Taghrid. Seven children in all, enough to fill their family home.

Isam dedicated himself to his family, his community, and his thriving chocolate business. But as 2010 drew to a close and Hadhad Chocolate prepared to start its twenty-fifth year in business, everything was about to come undone.

Two

In December 2010, a Tunisian man set himself on fire to protest his government's brutality, inspiring a reform movement that swept out the North African nation's authoritarian government. The following October, Tunisia held its first democratic elections. The Arab Spring spread to Egypt in early 2011, toppling the government in February. Morocco erupted into protests next, then Libya and Yemen. The kindling in all these countries was high unemployment, authoritarian governments, and desperation.

In February 2011, *Vogue* magazine printed a glowing profile of Bashar al-Assad and his wife, Asma. The magazine called Asma a "rose in the desert," gushed over her stylish clothes and her background in banking, and praised her and her husband for being "wildly democratic." The article called Syria the safest, most secular country in the Middle East, a place "without bombings, unrest or kidnappings." But Western reporters found the Syrian government had paid a publicity firm thousands of dollars to organize the interview and photo shoot. *Vogue* soon took the article offline and refused to comment on why it had run such a soft profile of a dictator who ruled with an iron fist. That same month, a teenager in the southern Syrian city of Daraa spray-painted "It's your turn, Doctor Bashar al-Assad" under the window of the principal's office at his school. Syrian security forces locked the graffiti artist in a room and hung him by his wrists, then whipped him with cables.

"I don't understand," he whimpered.

"Don't worry. You will," they answered. He named twenty-two classmates as co-conspirators, and the security forces detained all twenty-three schoolboys. They took the graffiti protester to Damascus. On his way into prison, he read on the wall: "Those who enter here are missing. Those who leave are newborn." In prison, guards forced him to beat other prisoners.

The families searched for the twenty-three missing boys. According to a newspaper account, a government minister told them, "Forget about your children. Go have new kids." The Syrian government marched soldiers through the streets. Small protests countered them in Damascus. In March 2011, the families marched in protest, throwing rocks at soldiers. Police opened fire and killed two people. Their families gathered to hold funerals. Police attended and shot several mourners dead.

Eventually, al-Assad's government freed the twenty-three boys. Daraa residents gathered at a mosque to celebrate their return. Soldiers stormed it, killing thirty-seven. Protests calling for al-Assad's downfall spread across Syria. Shootings escalated into mortar attacks and aerial bombardments. In July 2011, hundreds of thousands of ordinary Syrians marched against the government. Some armed themselves: first in defence, and then to attack. The government fought back.

The fighting reached Aleppo and Damascus in 2012. By June 2013, the United Nations counted ninety thousand dead. By August, a quarter of a million people were dead. Rockets filled with the nerve agent sarin exploded in Damascus's suburbs. Rebels said they were fired by the government; the government blamed the rebels.

Russia and Iran supported al-Assad. The United States, Canada, and France backed the rebels. The Islamic State seized land and claimed it for its growing caliphate. Some 4.5 million Syrians fled the country, heading for Lebanon, Jordan, Turkey, and Europe. Another 6.5 million Syrians fled internally. Only 21 million citizens remained.

Isam prayed the unrest would end. His factory now occupied three floors, and he employed dozens of people. By phone, Isam expanded into Aleppo and Homs, and then internationally into Lebanon, Iraq, and Jordan. One of his most popular products was a chocolate liquid that children loved to squirt on their breakfasts. Hadhad Chocolate had recently signed a deal to export into Europe, a huge step now in jeopardy.

On a spring day in 2012, Isam woke at 5 a.m. and slipped out of his sleeping house. He heard the distant sound of gunfire. As a boy, he'd played pickup soccer on this street. He and his friends pretended they represented Syria as it won its first World Cup, breaking up the game on the rare occasion when a car drove by. Isam still met with this same group of ten friends nearly every day to go to the mosque.

Isam and his friends entered the mosque to celebrate *Salat al-Fajr*, the prayer before sunrise. The *azan* called the faithful to prayer, reciting, "*Allahu Akbar*! God is Great!" Isam turned his heart toward God, the most merciful, most gracious, the master of the day of judgement.

"Verily, man is lost, except those that believe and do righteous good deeds, and recommend one another to the truth," he chanted with his brethren.

Some mornings, Isam and his friends would next visit the homes of those who had slept through morning prayer to give them a good-natured rousing. But today he drove directly to his factory. He passed through the military checkpoints without trouble. He arrived before anyone else and set down his cellphone in favour of the landline. He organized his work for the day, looking through his long lists of phone numbers. Many of his clients did not have cellphones, so Isam would call them at home, at work, at a friend's home, or at another family home to track them down. It was common to have ten phone numbers for one person.

A jumble of frantic messages gave him the news that the war had reached his home. Shahnaz told him a tank had been patrolling the neighbourhood and had shelled their house, either deliberately, as some kind of warning, or by mistake.

The extended Hadhad clan gathered at their damaged home to figure out what to do next. More than a few of their neighbours had already left. The Hadhad family had another, smaller house, in a safer neighbourhood of Damascus. That night, they reached an unbelievable conclusion: they would leave the old home and take refuge in the second house until the fighting stopped.

All of Isam and Shahnaz's children had been born in that ten-storey building. Many days Isam came home from work to find his children doing their homework around the big wooden table in the dining area, or sitting on the floor and watching television. Shahnaz would open the hand-crafted cabinetry to set the table. They ate together, on ordinary days and on holidays.

He remembered the first time he'd celebrated Mother's Day with Shahnaz. He could almost smell the baklava. The aunts and uncles had gathered in his home for the party. The women filled the table with dishes of tabbouleh, chicken, rice, fruit, and cake. All the nieces and nephews got gifts. The Hadhads had a tradition that every present was wrapped and handed out at random. The kids could unwrap a priceless toy or a worthless toothbrush. He remembered Tareq's disappointment one year when he unwrapped a Mickey Mouse doll.

In the morning, they packed a few bags and got in Isam's Volkswagen to drive to the safe house. Shahnaz glanced back at her bedroom window and hoped she would return soon. Those dreams were destroyed a few days later. One bachelor uncle, convinced the family was panicking over nothing, stayed behind. When the soldiers returned to the street, he stepped outside to greet them. They shot him dead and looted the house, storey by storey, and then set the building ablaze. The scorched house was left open to the elements. Tanks shelled it again, knocking out huge holes. Airstrikes rubbled it.

Thousands of anti-government rebels had poured into Damascus. Rumours said they planned to capture the capital and overthrow al-Assad. The rebels gained control over several districts and killed four government ministers. The government sent helicopter gunships and tanks onto the Damascus streets. Districts became war zones overnight. Rebels shot down a helicopter. Gunfire rattled the skies. The Free Syrian Army called it Operation Damascus Volcano; the government called it armed terrorism and promised to crush the uprising.

The Hadhad house had been one of the first hit in daytime fighting. The rebels boasted they would soon control the entire capital but found themselves hiding in private houses to escape the fury of the government. No one ever told the Hadhads why their home had been shelled, but it may have been wrongly marked as a rebel hideout. Western news outlets said it was the first time in Damascus that a ruler had turned his guns on the capital. From high on Mount Qasioun, artillery fire strafed the city below. The air stank with smoke and explosives. People fled the city in trucks, taxis, and cars. A revered military leader, Assef Shakwat, who had led the government crackdown since 2011, was killed in a bombing while he met with senior leaders in Damascus. The government held a funeral for him at the Tomb of the Unknown Soldier. Gunfire and explosions shook the air during the burial.

Poor rural men, heavily tanned from working the fields, picked up rebel guns and patrolled Damascus menacingly. Rebel leaders claimed they had fifteen thousand fighters in Damascus. They promised al-Assad was almost done. Al-Assad vowed he'd fight to the death.

The Hadhads, like many families, clung to the hope that this too would pass. Isam continued to work. Tareq attended medical classes at the university. Shahnaz kept the little house tidy and welcoming. The younger children finished their school year. Summer passed, bringing the hope that fall would return the world to peace.

On a cool November morning in 2012, workers trickled into the chocolate factory. War had become a part of life. Few people skipped work, as everyone wanted to make money while they could. Isam tried to carry on as usual. He met with his managers to oversee production, talked to the sales team about the market expansion, and discussed charitable giving with his family.

Isam sat at his desk, reading contracts, inventories, accounts, and anxious notes about the instability of the state. Tareq saw a news report about fighting on the edge of the industrial area and called his father to tell him. "Just be careful," he told his father. "If you can ask everyone to leave and close early, that would be good." Isam heard distant explosions. A family friend called Isam to tell him to leave: airstrikes were coming. Isam hung up and within minutes had shut down the factory and sent his workers home. He watched them all go before getting into his own car and driving downtown.

He was still driving ten minutes later when he heard explosions. He pressed the accelerator. Once home, he called some of his employees. Everyone was safe, but he could get no information about his factory. In news reports, the Syrian government said rebels were hiding in the industrial district.

His phone buzzed a few hours later. A friend had texted him photos from the industrial district, which had been bombed flat. Isam zoomed in on the images, searching the sea of concrete debris. He found the familiar area his chocolate factory occupied, though it was nearly unrecognizable. Only ruins remained.

Isam stared at the photos in silence. Looking at the rubble where his factory once stood, he felt something crumbling inside. Everything he'd known, everything he'd worked for, was gone. They couldn't go back to the ten-storey home. His factory was destroyed. Like most Syrians, he didn't use banks and kept his money in safes in his house and factory. The safes and the life's savings they'd contained were gone. He'd poured himself into his business for twenty-seven years, building it from a one-person factory into a giant company that reached across the region. He had nothing left but his family, and he was terrified the war would take them, too.

Isam could not speak for three days. One horror followed swiftly on another. Isam's cousin Bassam lived with his wife and young children in one of Damascus's southern suburbs. Although other relatives had left and had urged him to do the same, he was determined to stay, insisting that he would rather die in the house where he was born. In early 2013, a tank rumbled down his street. Bassam went out to the balcony. Soldiers were going from house to house, ostensibly looking for rebels but, in reality, grabbing anyone they saw.

"Why did someone leave their car in the middle of the road?" a soldier complained loudly. "We need to get all this equipment through." He was talking about Bassam's car, a car he'd long saved for and which was his family's surest means of escape if he changed his mind about fleeing. Bassam watched the soldiers set the car on fire, and he told his wife he was going to go downstairs, put the fire out, and move the car. She put their children in the bathroom for safety and then watched from the balcony while Bassam went down to the street.

Bassam approached the soldiers with open hands and a friendly posture. "I'm not a rebel. I just want to put the fire out," he told one soldier.

"You want your car?" the soldier asked.

"Yes," he replied.

"Come with us."

Bassam and three other men were lined up against a wall. A soldier asked the first man what he wanted. "I want my house," he replied. They shot him dead.

"What do you want?" they asked the terrified second man.

"I just want to get out of here! I'm a civilian."

They shot him, too.

"What do you want?" they asked Bassam.

"I don't want anything. Just don't do anything," he pleaded. "I want to go back to my family."

"No," the soldier said. "You said you want your car."

And he shot Bassam in the head.

When the Hadhads heard about Bassam's murder, it opened a torrent of grief. They could only wonder how much longer any of them would be safe in Damascus.

❖

Tareq's head slammed into the sidewalk. He studied the dust floating in the spring air. People were running all over the street, scrambling for their houses, trying to escape. *Am I dead?*

Weeks earlier, his mother, sensing that something bad was about to happen, had called him home from university, and moments later rockets had hit the school and killed several students. But he had survived, and just that morning he'd returned to university to attend a memorial for the dead students. Then he'd walked to his family's temporary home, where the Hadhads shared the second floor. His little brother, Ahmad, was cleaning the family car on the street. Tareq stopped and asked Ahmad if he had made any friends in the new neighbourhood yet. And then the rocket exploded.

Realizing that he was not dead, Tareq staggered to his feet. Ahmad, only nine years old, lay with his eyes wide open, staring at the sky.

"Ahmad, please, can you say something?" Tareq begged. "I need to make sure you are alive!" Ahmad said nothing. "Ahmad! Please say something, do something!" Finally, his little brother moved his hand. They were both in shock and wounded, but not fatally.

Shahnaz had been outside on the balcony, watching her two sons in the street. The blast blew her back inside the house. She scrambled to her feet and staggered to the balcony to see her two sons lying on the ground. When she saw them moving, she began waving frantically and screaming at them to come home. To Tareq, it seemed that she only mouthed the words. She raced downstairs and opened the door to pull them in.

"Are you okay?" she asked. This time Tareq could hear her. She led her sons upstairs to patch up their cuts and clean the dust off them.

The extended Hadhad clan gathered in the basement that evening. Helicopters chopped the sky and planes dropped bombs that screamed through the air and shook the ground when they exploded. Soldiers marched through the streets hunting for rebels. The Hadhads had brought water and food into the cramped basement, but they wouldn't last long. Dozens of family members were squished into the small basement day and night, with only one window offering a glimpse outside. They kept it closed and covered so that no soldier would see the light and investigate.

The war raged outside for a full week. The Hadhads cowered in the basement. No one could go to school, to work, to the store, or even upstairs. Finally, the families started to talk about leaving.

"Should we stay and give our lives in Syria another chance?" someone asked.

"And wait for one of us to become the next victim?" another countered.

Nothing kept you safe in Syria. A steady stream of cousins, aunts, and uncles fled for Jordan, Lebanon, Egypt, and Turkey, many passing through this same house.

Batoul, their second-youngest daughter, did not want to go. She was fifteen and loved living in the big city. She adored her school. Even during the war, she rarely missed a class. She studied Arabic, English, and French, and math and science, too. She excelled as a student. Before the war, her father would pick her up after school and drive her home. She'd eat a late lunch before he returned and took her to the factory, where she'd help make the boxes of chocolate or package the liquid chocolate that made up so much of their business. It was important work, she was learning about the business, and she enjoyed the time with her father.

On days off, she'd head to the glimmering shopping malls, or maybe wander around Damascus's Old City and chat with shopkeepers who'd claim their first sale was to Adam and Eve back in the Garden of Eden days. She mostly shopped with her sisters or cousins. Clothes were always the main target. She couldn't imagine her life being better elsewhere.

But when the war started, when it scorched the edges of Damascus, she understood things were well out of her control. It was the sound that convinced her: the huge explosions that shook the air. She flinched each time she heard a crash. Her fear and sorrow sank deeper and darker. She felt something was dying.

"We are not staying, absolutely," Tareq said in a firm voice. "Not for another day."

"Where shall we go?" someone asked.

"It doesn't matter where we go. We should go to a place where we are safe," Tareq said. "That's what life is about: to be in a peaceful place, to know you will not be arrested and killed, you will not be shot, you will not be executed. You will not have a roof collapse on your head. You will not hear explosions. Where at the end of the day, you won't hide from airstrikes and bombing. It's not time to do business, it's not time to do medicine. It's time to survive."

As the night wore on, the agonizing discussion turned to counting the number of family members who had been arrested by the government, hurt by bombs and airstrikes, or rendered homeless by street fighting. A cousin had been kidnapped for a $1.5 million ransom, a ridiculous demand in a country where a wealthy person might have $500,000. The bachelor uncle killed in the street outside the family home. Bassam, shot dead against a wall.

In the darkest hour of the night, the Hadhads agreed to flee at dawn. Some would try to get to Egypt. Others would go to Jordan. Isam's family would head for Lebanon. As the Hadhads prepared to leave the great city for the last time, the city lights crawled up the foothill of Mount Qasioun, where the flower *Iris damascena* bloomed on the eastern flank and nowhere else on Earth.

They passed a fitful final night. Tareq realized this could be the last sunrise he ever saw in the city his family had called home as far back as anyone could remember. The rest of his family awoke, ate a quick breakfast, prayed, and prepared for flight.

"We must leave anything that could pose a risk," Shahnaz said.

In Syria at that moment, that could be almost anything. People weren't allowed to just leave the country. Everyone had to pose as tourists, as people visiting family, as people with business appointments. The Hadhads took only the clothes they wore and a few spares. The once-prosperous family carried only three hundred thousand Syrian pounds, the equivalent of around $800. Shahnaz tried to reassure everyone. "We will not be away so long," she promised. "One month and the war will end and we will come back."

Seven family members—Isam, Shahnaz, Walaa, Tareq, Batoul, Ahmad, and Taghrid—jammed themselves into Isam's old Volkswagen, which was one of the last things the family owned. Isam and Shahnaz's two eldest daughters would remain in Damascus with their husbands and families.

Shahnaz's father accompanied them. He ran a busy clothing store in Damascus, a place where Shahnaz often worked, and was the only member of the family who had been outside Syria. The Hadhads hoped his experience would prove useful to them in their first days in Lebanon. He planned to return to Damascus once his daughter and her family were settled.

Batoul silently watched her city through the car windows. Tears rolled down her face. Damascus was her whole heart. She didn't want to leave, but she could see the war was destroying everything.

It would usually take ninety minutes to drive from Damascus to Lebanon, but the maze of checkpoints manned by soldiers made the journey unpredictable. Isam grew worried that Tareq, his military-aged son, could too easily be seen sitting by the window. "Sit in the middle," he said. Tareq folded his long legs and sat in the middle of the backseat, flanked by his sisters and younger brother.

Problems started at the first checkpoint.

"How old is your son?" a soldier asked.

"Don't worry about him. He's fine," Isam said.

The soldiers insisted on seeing Tareq's military book. The document records all military service for all Syrian men or their reasons for not serving. Tareq's medical studies exempted him from duty, but many soldiers ignored such rules.

"It's better for you to come back to the country," the soldier said. "It will not be yours if you don't come back shortly."

Isam assured him they would be back soon, thanked him, and drove on. The checkpoint soldiers grew nastier as they drove out of the city. Any man aged eighteen to forty could be conscripted into military service. The Hadhads watched soldiers pull young men out of vehicles and separate them from their families. The tension in the car increased with each turn of its wheels.

Finally, they drew near the border with Lebanon.

"This is the last checkpoint. If we survive this, we're ninety per cent out of the country," Tareq said.

They watched soldiers order young men off a bus in front of them. The young men were told to stand in the rain. The Hadhads reached the checkpoint.

"I'm not driving you through," Isam said to Tareq. "They will ask you to leave the car."

"We don't have any other option," Tareq replied. "If we turn around and go back to the city, they will know that something is wrong. They might even shoot everyone in the car."

Isam steeled his nerve and rolled down the window. "Hey, guys," he called out. "We just have an urgent appointment in Lebanon. We really have to pass."

The soldiers did not answer. They eyed Tareq. Isam reached for his wad of bills and gave half of it—about $400—to one soldier. He pocketed it and let them through. The actual border lay just ahead. The border guards were more professional than the checkpoint soldiers, but still they pressed the Hadhads, wanting to know why this young man was leaving the country.

"We are legal. We are just going for a short stay, and then we will come back," Isam said. The guards told them to wait. Morning became afternoon, and afternoon turned into evening. The Hadhads watched as thousands of Syrians funnelled through the border. Finally, at eight o'clock, the Hadhads were waved forward, and Isam drove his family out of Syria.

At the Lebanese border, they found another long line of Syrians waiting to be processed. The Lebanese officials were overwhelmed. The Hadhads waited while guards searched their luggage.

"Welcome to Lebanon," a border official said, waving them into the country.

"We are safe," Tareq said quietly.

They arrived in Lebanon late in the evening. Isam parked on the side of the street in the first city they entered. "Where should we go?" he asked. No one answered. This was the end of the plan.

The weary family looked out the dirty car windows at the quiet streets of a city holding one hundred thousand strangers. The car was all they owned. They had very little cash left. It was so late at night, and so many fleeing Syrians were looking for shelter, that they were unlikely to find room in any inn, and they couldn't afford one, anyway.

Leaving had been dangerous, but turning back to Damascus now would be suicidal. The heat faded from the car, replaced by the chilly night air. The windows fogged up. The Hadhads remained in the Volkswagen, squished against each other, shivering. They nodded over their knees as sleep overcame them. *God, what are we doing?* they wondered.

Three

The Hadhads woke from their uneasy first night in Lebanon, stretching as much as the Volkswagen would allow. Shahnaz and Isam tried to think of a next step. They had brought their children out of danger. Now they must find safety.

Losing his home, his business, and now his country seemed to have killed a part of Isam. Tareq had never seen his father so afraid, and a moment of despair took hold.

No one wanted to spend another night homeless on the streets of a strange city.

Finally, as dawn warmed the air, Shahnaz asked her father about his student days in Damascus decades earlier. Hadn't he made a Lebanese friend? He nodded and recalled a name he'd not thought of in years: Bassam. Details about Bassam came back to him. The friendship had largely ended when they graduated fifty years ago, but they had had intermittent contact when Shahnaz's father travelled for business. He didn't know Bassam's phone number, email, or address, but he did know his ancestral home: the Beqaa Valley in fertile eastern Lebanon.

It was the only lead they had. Shahnaz's father would not make the journey. Having guided his daughter out of immediate danger, he was anxious to return to Damascus to be with the rest of his family.

They hugged, kissed, and cried. They prayed they would see each other again. Isam started the Volkswagen and began the drive north.

As they entered the Beqaa Valley, Isam kept pulling over, rolling down his window, and asking people if they knew Bassam. No one did. Isam did this over and over, until finally one man's eyes lit up. He not only knew Bassam, but they lived very close to each other. He was willing to show the Hadhads the way.

The Hadhads exchanged smiles as the man climbed into the Volkswagen. He chatted with them about their journey and their connection to Bassam. To the neighbour, showing them the way to Bassam's house was just a small courtesy in a busy day, but the Hadhads would see him as one of the ways God was helping them to safety, and they would hold him in their prayers.

The valley town overflowed with Syrian refugees. People were staying in offices, stores, mosques, and churches. Bassam's front yard resembled a refugee camp. He knew many Syrians, and he was too kind to turn anyone away. He wasn't home when the Hadhads arrived, but they waited until he returned. He welcomed them to what shelter he could offer. The family slept well that night.

Lebanon has a population of six million people. Roughly a million Syrians had entered since 2011, and the country was struggling to cope. It would soon close the border to further refugees, and Syrians already in Lebanon would have to pay for a residency permit every six months. They would not be allowed to work, to attend public schools, or to access Lebanon's hospitals. Many of the Syrian refugees lived in makeshift homes built in informal settlements. Almost all of them lived in poverty, as did many Lebanese.

The Hadhads did not want to become refugees. The family called the certificate of refugee the "certificate of non-belonging." It was an official declaration that they had absolutely nothing. But Tareq realized that if they didn't register, his family would have no status at all. Reluctantly, they went to the United Nations High Commissioner for Refugees office in Beqaa Valley to fill out the required paperwork. A clerk gave them each a number, printed it on a piece of paper, and told them to pin the numbers to their chests. They did so, sat in a hallway with other refugees, and waited to be called for an interview.

An official called out a number, but no one rose. The number was called again. People started glancing at each other's chests to see whose number it was. After the third time, the official stood in front of Tareq.

"It's your number, sir," he said. "Why are you not replying?"

"Because I am not a number," Tareq replied. "I don't want to remember these four or five digits my entire life. I have a name. You could have taken our names and called us by name."

Shahnaz tried to calm her upset son. He was scaring the younger children. Tareq's anger surprised his family. He had calmly organized the interviews, gotten them to the building, and seated them—and now he was erupting at this official, fighting back tears.

The United Nations certified the Hadhad family as refugees. The status gave them certain international protections and meant the United Nations would try to find a country that would accept them. It also gave them a relief parcel but no cash and no place to stay while they waited. Lebanon had not signed the UN's 1951 Refugee Convention, and later that year the country would stop letting Syrians register as refugees.

They decided not to go to the informal refugee camps but to find their own way. They asked both friends and strangers for leads on places to stay. Someone would whisper that a person living at a certain address had an empty room and might let them stay there. They would go, stay for as long as they could, perhaps two weeks, and then learn of another whispered destination. Another helpful person—a Lebanese, a Syrian—would say, "Go to this address. The owner does not live there and does not care about the property. You can stay awhile."

They mostly drifted along Lebanon's border with Syria. Like a mother visiting the grave, they looked over to Syria and wept. They struggled to sleep at night. When it was quiet, they could hear the bombs exploding in Homs. At times, missiles accidentally flew past the border and smashed into Lebanon. The ironic possibility of dying in the Syrian war while in Lebanon troubled them.

Isam got a text from the United Nations a few weeks later telling him his relief parcel was ready. He collected it and brought it to his wife and children. Inside they discovered food and toothbrushes. Isam felt a flush of shame. He, the person who had once given generous donations to the needy, was reduced to accepting donated food and toiletries. He gave most of the items to Syrian refugees who needed them more.

"Let's go back to Damascus," Batoul pleaded, sick at the thought of spending her teenage years on the run. "We're not going to be okay in Lebanon."

"No," Shahnaz said. "If we go back to Damascus, we would not be safe."

"We would be safe in Damascus," Batoul countered. "We can't find an apartment or house to live in here."

"Batoul, you have to wait."

The one thing they had in abundance in Lebanon was time: time to replay terrifying memories, time to mourn their ruined home, time to feel bitter about the destroyed chocolate factory. They woke, endured the day, and tried to sleep again. They relied on gifts from their growing network of new friends. As time passed, people started seeking them out to offer help. Some were Syrians who had been in the country for a long time, others were Lebanese people who had fled to Syria during their own war. They remembered how Syria had opened its doors to them, and now they were determined to do the same. Whatever the maps said, many felt as though Lebanon and Syria were one country, and that citizens of one country should not be refugees in the other.

Weeks dragged past. Tareq grew restless. He asked himself how he could turn devastation into opportunity. He had heard that the United Nations used volunteers to help with its mobile medical clinic. Tareq had nearly completed his medical studies in Damascus; it deeply upset him to have had the stethoscope snatched from his neck just before he could graduate, and he was eager to prove himself. He went to the UN building and stopped the first employee he saw.

He introduced himself as a medical student. "Can I get any volunteering work with you?" he asked. "I really want to get out of where I am right now: nowhere. I want to be active. I know how to do it. I know how to consult the patients. I know how to deliver records to the supervisor of the shift. I can do assessments and medical surveillance in the camps."

"Yes, you can help out," the employee said. He explained that the clinic, which was just a car packed with medical supplies, covered much of northern Lebanon. Staff travelled to Syrian refugees, some living in tents, some in rooms in homes like the Hadhads, and gave them basic medical treatment.

Tareq turned up at 5 a.m. the next day. On his first field trip, he saw that many families had it much worse than his. He met widows, orphans, and grieving fathers. He treated a patient with an infection that would otherwise have killed him in weeks. In the weeks that followed, he developed awareness programs to protect against certain vicious diseases and taught the refugees living in the crowded camps the hygienic practices that would help keep them healthy. He informed them of their legal rights, too, and he found time to raise money for supplies. He had seen children die of diarrhea because they could not buy the medication that could stop it.

"Why should I play the role of victim?" Tareq asked himself. "I can help all of these people in the camps with whatever I can."

Tareq found purpose in treating those in misery. He drew inspiration from his patients' strength. Work left no time to dwell on the past or worry about the future. He spoke better English than most and became a trusted translator for NGOs and health clinics. He helped write to donors who could find a hospital bed or pay medical bills. He saw his family as often as he could, and he brought his good cheer home with him. Moving from house to house, they seemed to forever repeat the same eventless day. Shahnaz worried about keeping her family intact. They talked to Kenana and Alaa, still with their husbands and young children in Damascus. Isam sank into depression. He was not alone.

Nadim Almoshmosh, a psychiatrist who worked with Syrian refugees, would later observe that many of them left the country with a belief that their absence would be temporary. They started out resilient and defiant, determined to endure this time of difficulty before they inevitably returned to their happier, more comfortable lives in Syria. But as the war dragged on and days turned into months and months into years, people fell into despair and hopelessness. Increasingly dependent on charity and food vouchers, Almoshmosh noted, they felt humiliated and trapped. Once-confident men, suddenly unable to support either themselves or their families, lost their identity and grew disoriented. Their children, who had always been able to count on them, and who had been ripped from their schools and friends, felt anxious and insecure. People felt guilty about the loved ones they'd left behind in Syria and worried they'd be killed. Many were vulnerable to exploitation in the refugee camps, as they had no power, no money, and nowhere else to turn.

Reluctant to share their feelings, many of the refugees pushed their pain inward and suffered silently.

Once the Hadhads accepted that their temporary stay in Lebanon would last indefinitely, they found a cramped three-room apartment in Saida, a beautiful port town that was as old as Damascus. Thousands of years ago, Saida's citizens traded with mighty Egypt, and the town was famed around the world for its glass-making industry. The Phoenicians had decorated their trading city with thick citrus trees and fragrant banana groves. Today, vendors selling fresh fruit and sweets — most famously a crumbly cookie called *senioura* — filled the ancient *souq*'s narrow lanes, tunnels, and buildings.

Shahnaz had developed a wide support network, and she drew from it to help her find the apartment. She learned of the apartment's existence from neighbours who were part of a sort of Lebanese Underground Railway, ordinary citizens who wanted to help Syrians, regardless of what the Lebanese government did or did not do. They also helped the Hadhads furnish the apartment as well as they could.

They tried to get back to something like a normal life. No one could legally work, but they needed money. Isam started hiring himself out for odd jobs. He briefly tried making chocolate, but his heart wasn't in it. He even stopped eating chocolate. Shahnaz enrolled her children in a local school, which would teach them math, science, and English. Walaa was engaged to a man who worked in Saudi Arabia and would soon leave to marry him and live in that country.

Batoul enjoyed the newfound stability. She wanted to resume her studies and to hang out with other teenage girls. She made many Syrian and Lebanese friends, and she felt she was getting her life back. They studied together, told jokes, and went shopping. Her friends helped her when she struggled. The teachers valued their students and put long hours into helping the girls become bright, capable adults. Batoul, thinking about her future, asked her teachers about university. She imagined herself moving somewhere exciting, like Beirut.

The illusion of peace was shattered with a phone call in March 2014, a year into their time as refugees. It was Alaa. She spoke rapidly, her voice choked with fear. The night before, government security forces had broken into her apartment. The soldiers grabbed her husband, Mamdouh, and his two brothers, hauling them out of the apartment and into waiting vehicles. The cars tore off into the night. It was over in minutes. Now Alaa was left alone with their young children.

Alaa said she had no idea if Mamdouh and his brothers had been killed, if they were being tortured in a prison dungeon somewhere in Damascus, or if the soldiers would realize they'd detained innocent men and release them that afternoon. Four-year-old Omar, just old enough to be aware that members of his family kept disappearing, cried constantly. Two-year-old Sana barely understood what was happening.

The Hadhads had to make another urgent decision. Should Alaa stay in Damascus at the apartment in case Mamdouh was released? Would the security forces return and abduct her too? And who would look after their children if that happened? If she left, Mamdouh might never find her and their children. If she stayed, they all might die.

Thousands of ordinary Syrians disappeared during the war. Many were locked in filthy cells and tortured. Amnesty International reported numerous cases in which innocent people were snatched off the streets and held for months before being freed. One young man died of a heart attack in the cells. Mothers were locked up with children as young as two. Many of the disappeared were simply never heard from again.

Alaa decided to make a run for the border. Tareq told her to pose as a tourist. He booked her a hotel in Beirut so she could prove she and the children were visiting. Alaa packed a few bags and started the dangerous bus journey to Lebanon. Luckily, the soldiers at the checkpoints paid little attention to her, and she and her children crossed into Lebanon. Tareq was waiting for them on the other side of the border and drove them to Saida. Brother and sister were happy to be together again, but worry for Mamdouh and his brothers overshadowed the reunion. Nine people now shared the three-room apartment.

❖

On a field trip with the mobile clinic, Tareq unexpectedly ran into a beloved face: his fourth-cousin Hanan from Homs. They shared the same great-great-great-grandparents. Hanan was with two of her young children. As Tareq wrapped his long arms around them, he noticed one child was missing, as was her husband. Hanan explained that back in Syria, her husband went shopping for food and didn't come home. She had stayed up all night waiting for him. Her husband was an engineer. He had no involvement with either the military or the rebels. When he didn't return, Hanan figured he'd been arrested and spent what money she had trying to find him. Wealthy people could pay huge sums for information about a son or husband disappeared into the prisons; the poor would never know. Whatever she paid was not enough: Hanan learned nothing. Eventually, she lost hope that he would ever come back and took her children to Lebanon.

Hanan hoped Lebanon would be a place of safety, but when she overstayed her permit she was arrested and imprisoned for a month. One of her three children died in a fire while she was incarcerated.

"I'm not staying in Lebanon," she told Tareq. "I can't afford to lose the other two kids. I'm going to Turkey."

"What are you going to do in Turkey?"

"Find a way to Europe. I can't wait for the UN to interview me, then settle us in another country."

Tareq was frightened for her. He knew that finding another way to Europe most likely meant paying a people smuggler. But he couldn't talk her out of it. They parted, promising to keep in touch. Weeks later, his phone buzzed with the news that she was in Turkey. She hoped to get to Germany. When Tareq told his family about Hanan, they wanted to join her. Tareq insisted that it was too dangerous. A few days later Hanan texted him the news that she had paid smugglers to take her and her children to Greece; they were already on the boat.

"Text me every 15 minutes so I know you're fine," Tareq replied.

"OK—so long as there is coverage," she texted back.

Tareq clutched his phone that night and tried to sleep. He called and texted his cousin, but she did not answer. He told himself her phone battery had died. He contacted mutual friends, but they had no news, either. He checked a Facebook page that shared information about Syrians. Nothing.

When morning finally came, it brought dreadful news. A smuggler's boat, meant to carry fifteen people but packed with dozens of refugees, had sailed for Lesbos on rough seas. A trip that would have taken ninety minutes on one of the tourist ferries took hours. Safety floated into sight as Lesbos's shore rose over the horizon. But something went wrong on the boat, and in seconds everyone was in the cold water. There were no life jackets. Some began swimming to shore; others searched desperately in the water for something to cling to. The strong dragged themselves through the waves and crawled onto the beach. Hanan and her two children were not among the strong. They drowned together. Fifty people lost their lives.

Tareq was sick with grief for his cousin and her children. He knew many friends who had died the same way. The futility of life in Lebanon could drive desperate and frustrated Syrians to ignore the dangers and try to cross the Mediterranean. Here, his sisters and brother were sometimes harassed on the streets. His father could not work openly and had been detained by Lebanese security forces several times, the last time for getting groceries. He'd always been released quickly, but one day he might not come home. Tareq worried that his parents would take the family to Turkey and find a smuggler in Izmir. They, too, could squeeze onto an overloaded boat. Those who made it to the other side were not much better off than those who didn't. Where would they go? Another refugee camp? Another number pinned to their chests?

Tareq realized that he couldn't help others while his family suffered. He was only twenty-two years old, but he knew that it was his responsibility to get them out of Lebanon and settled somewhere truly safe.

Tareq urged his family not to take their chances with the smugglers. They must stick to the United Nations and the proper channels. Eventually they could be resettled in Europe or even North America. Again and again he told his family to be patient. Everything would work out for them. Life would give them another chance.

Four

Tareq hailed a late-night taxi to drive him from the mobile medical clinic's office in Beirut to his family's small apartment in Saida, forty kilometres south along the Mediterranean coast. It was January 2015, and the news lately had been increasingly dire. Mortar fire had hit a Damascus school, killing eleven children. Rebels had captured the southern city of Nawa from the government. The Islamic State had shot down a Syrian fighter plane. Government airstrikes on Raqqa had killed one hundred civilians. The national air force bombed a Damascus suburb and killed forty-two people, including six children, and claimed they had killed rebels. The United Nations counted two hundred thousand Syrian dead as the war entered its fifth year.

"Where are you from, man?" the driver asked him.

"Syria," he answered. They spoke briefly about the life Tareq had left behind.

"Would you like to continue your studies?" the driver asked him. "One of my passengers this morning told me the Canadian embassy is offering scholarships for you guys, the Syrian students. If you have an interest, you can go there."

When they reached Saida, the driver refused to accept payment, saying he lived nearby and was heading home anyway when Tareq flagged him down. As Tareq walked down the lanes leading to his family's apartment, he noticed a Canadian flag hanging on a front door. It seemed an omen. He'd never thought about Canada before. The only images it brought to mind were Mounties and snow.

He climbed the stairs to the apartment and found the older members of his family waiting for him. It was hard to believe they all fit. He hugged Alaa, keeping quiet so as to not wake the younger children. It had been nine months since Alaa's husband had vanished, and she still had no idea if he was dead or alive. Shahnaz smiled and welcomed him home. She was the fireplace they all warmed themselves around: wherever she was, she could make it their home. Isam asked him about his work. Batoul smiled shyly and told him about her school and friends.

They sat up for a while in the living room. They could not stay in Lebanon, yet there was nowhere for them to go. The year before, 2014, had produced more refugees than any year on the United Nations' record. The UN's High Commissioner for Refugees counted sixty million displaced people, half of whom were children. It was the worst it had been since the end of World War II. António Guterres, the head of the UNHCR, called it a "completely chaotic situation" that had caused a "staggering escalation of human suffering, because each displaced person is a tragic story." Syria alone had forced out nearly four million refugees, making almost one out of every five Syrians a refugee. The number of people looking for a safe haven overwhelmed Middle Eastern and European countries.

The Hadhads had been official refugees for nearly two years, but they still had no options for resettlement. In Lebanon, they had to find extra money to renew their residency permit every six months, and they could not work, could not attend university, and could never become citizens.

Isam and Shahnaz talked to Tareq late into the night before finally falling asleep. Everyone slept on the floor, as they had no beds, only a couch and a chair. Tareq lay awake and started to think seriously about Canada. He realized it had left a deeper impression on him than just mounted police and snow. Somehow, he knew that Canada valued immigrants, that it took in refugees, and that people could keep their own identity even as they became part of the bigger national character. He had a vague sense that Canada was a quieter, less boastful place than the United States and that it valued hard-working people who wanted to get ahead.

Tareq used his phone to search for the organization the taxi driver had told him about: the World University Service of Canada, or WUSC. He found an application and used up his data to fill it out. The taxi driver had gotten it right: if Tareq won a student visa, he could move to Canada and become a doctor. Since he had only a few months or a year left in his Syrian studies, he figured he could become a doctor fairly quickly. He also saw that Canada needed doctors, especially in rural areas. Once he got a foothold, he thought, he could bring the rest of his family over. From what he read online, though, that would take another five years. That would mean that even if he somehow reached Canada that year, his family would have to survive as refugees until 2020.

He put down his phone. His eyes were getting tired. Filling out the WUSC application had a similar effect to buying a lottery ticket: he didn't expect anything to happen, but it was fun to think about a brighter future for a little while. Tareq lulled himself to sleep. He'd have to be up again in a few hours to catch a taxi back to Beirut.

For weeks Tareq heard nothing about his application. He never mentioned it to his family and eventually he even forgot about it. But one day he was in Beirut, helping his team prepare for the next field trip. He was checking off the supply lists and gathering information about the sick people they hoped to treat when his phone rang. The number was hidden.

"*Marhaba*?" he said. "Hello?"

"Tareq?" a man asked in Arabic.

"Yes, this is Tareq."

"Oh! This is the Canadian embassy. Congratulations! I was really impressed with your application. Can you attend an inter—"

Tareq hung up. It was almost certainly a scammer blocking his number to prevent detection. (He only later realized it was his own phone's settings that accidentally hid the number.) Then he received an email following up on the phone call, and the address looked legitimate. After that, he received a second email, this time from a woman who claimed to work for WUSC. She seemed to have read his application, so he agreed to meet for an interview at the Canadian embassy.

Two months later, he emptied his pockets and walked through the metal detector. Security told him he'd have to leave his phone and wristwatch with them. Friendly Lebanese and Canadian staff welcomed him and took him to the interview room. He met five other young Syrian men vying for the same WUSC opportunity. All were in good cheer, thrilled at the prospect of an escape. They tried to figure out what the Canadians were looking for from them. They talked about what to say of their pasts and their hopes for the future. They exchanged phone numbers and wished each other good luck.

Tareq took a deep breath when his turn came. He smiled widely and said hello to everyone inside the room. The WUSC staff told him they could get him into an undergraduate program in Canada. His face fell. He had already completed many years of medical studies, and the thought of starting from scratch crushed his spirits.

"Well, I'm not going to get an undergraduate degree again. I can't. I want to be a physician," he said.

Saying no would mean he was turning down what was likely his only chance to go to Canada. Tareq said no.

One of the staff in the room was Natalie Jewett. Her husband had been posted to the Canadian embassy in Beirut in 2014, and the Canadian government had found a position for her, too, helping

WUSC with its refugee settlement program. They brought their nine-year-old daughter, who soon grew tired of hearing her parents tell her how lucky she was to be Canadian.

The Canadian embassy in Beirut was housed in a ten-storey building with uninterrupted views of the Mediterranean Sea out the back windows. The front faced the multi-lane Coastal Highway that ran through the Jal el Dib neighbourhood. The busy road separated the embassy from the burger joints, banks, churches, mosques, and ice cream parlours of Beirut's seaside. The embassy was a target for militants and fanatics, so security was always tight.

Before Tareq's interview, Natalie had reviewed his application. She read about his medical background and the volunteer work he'd been doing with the mobile clinic. She learned how his family had been forced from Syria. So many of the Syrians she'd encountered seemed like broken lamps glued together. His exuberant praise for Canada and his determination to make the best of himself shone on the screen. She could imagine him doing well in Canada. She filed his application with the others she'd earmarked as "best ones."

Now, despite watching Tareq politely but firmly decline the chance to start over from the beginning, she became convinced he could do something special in Canada. She spoke to her manager, Oscar Jacobs, and made a case for the applicants she felt were particularly promising, including Tareq.

"How can we help these kids?" she asked. "They're so great, so smart. I've rarely met a nineteen- or twenty-year-old that is so accomplished, selfless, community minded, and family minded. How can we help?"

Oscar was the immigration program manager. The career diplomat had worked for the Canadian government on many immigration and refugee issues around the world. The wars in Iraq and Syria had forced Canada to shut its offices in Baghdad and Damascus, so Beirut handled the 200,000 Iraqi refugees who had fled that country's war, along with the 450,000 Palestinian refugees in Lebanon, some of whom had been stateless since the foundation of Israel in 1948.

Oscar looked over Tareq's application. Super impressive, Oscar thought. There were so many impressive refugees. The young students brimmed with enthusiasm and earnestness. But Oscar thought about Tareq Hadhad and decided to do what he could to find him a path to Canada.

Tareq, meanwhile, had left the embassy believing that his bid to make a new life in Canada was over. But a few months later, he received an email from a Canadian immigration official. The email told Tareq that he and some other applicants were being offered the opportunity to emigrate to Canada with their families and invited him to an information session. Tareq tidied himself up, pulled on his brown leather jacket, and went back to the embassy. When he arrived, he found that the other Syrians he had met at his first interview had also been summoned back.

A cheerful official told them that Canada was willing to issue them visas that would permit them and their families to travel to Canada immediately. "Any place in Canada you want," he said. Then he addressed them individually, asking each in turn if they wanted to go to Canada. "This is real guys," he promised as the Syrians broke down in simultaneous laughter and tears. "Why are you laughing?"

Tareq struggled to regain his composure. "It's very weird to ask us if we are interested," he explained. "Of course we are interested to leave the country in any way!"

The official told them to go home and prepare to leave within weeks.

It was time to talk to his family about Canada, but first Tareq celebrated with a group selfie he posted to his Instagram account. Then he called Isam. "Dad, I'm coming tonight. There's so much sweet news. Don't sleep."

The entire neighbourhood was dark and still when he arrived home, but lights blazed in the Hadhad apartment. His entire family stood in the foyer, waiting for him. They'd spent the time since he called wondering what he was so excited about. Had he gotten a new job? A better home? Safe passage to Europe?

"*Enteh mneh?*" Isam asked. "Are you fine? Is there anything that has happened today?"

Tareq revelled in the moment. "Well, Dad, we will travel." His family cheered.

"Where? To Germany?" Shahnaz asked. Tareq shook his head.

"Sweden?" tried his father. No.

"The United States?" asked Batoul. Grinning, Tareq said no again.

"Canada!" he finally said. Their faces fell.

"Canada is too cold!" they protested. "It's the coldest country on Earth! How are we going to survive there? We need maybe ten jackets each just to get warm."

Batoul knew this would mean she couldn't go to university in Lebanon. She would, again, be parted from her friends. She would turn sixteen on July 1, and she pictured herself celebrating alone on an ice floe.

"Canada is the best country. You will continue your studies there," Tareq told her.

They quickly warmed to the idea of a new chance at life.

April arrived. The family was sure it was their last April in Lebanon. They began learning all they could about Canada. They made regular trips to the now familiar embassy in Beirut for a flurry of medical tests and endless paperwork. April ended. May passed. June started. July 1 came and Batoul turned sixteen, still in Lebanon.

The Canadians at the embassy looked discouraged and couldn't explain the delay. Frustrated, three of the other Syrians who had been promised speedy migration paid smugglers to take them through Turkey to Europe. Again the Hadhads gave some thought to doing the same.

On August 2, Canadian Prime Minister Stephen Harper called a federal election. A week later he promised to bring 10,000 Syrian refugees to Canada. His government had already let 2,500 in since the war started. But no one at the embassy called the Hadhads.

Tareq did get a call from the United Nations, asking if he would accept an opportunity to go to France instead. A year earlier, the Hadhads would have said *oui* at once. But that was before the Canada option. Tareq checked with his family. No one seemed eager to go to France. His mother put her foot down.

"We really don't want to go to France," Shahnaz said. "We've spent the last months learning about Canada, and how impressive this country is, how amazing it is. The people, the welcome, the diversity. Wherever we stay in Canada, we will find people from different parts of the world. We won't be successful in France."

The Hadhads said no to France, shutting the only open door out of Lebanon.

The world changed a few weeks later on September 2 when a toddler washed up on a Turkish shore. Two-year-old Alan Kurdi's family had fled Syria hoping to join family in Canada. Sixteen people had climbed into an eight-person inflatable boat and pushed off, hoping to travel just four kilometres to Kos, Greece. They barely made it off the shore before the engine failed and the boat capsized. Alan drowned, as did his mother and brother. His father survived. Oxfam reported that 4,664 people had drowned in similar circumstances in the preceding twelve months.

A Reuters journalist captured photos of Alan Kurdi's body lying on the beach and the moment a police officer picked him up. An estimated twenty million people viewed the images on social media. US President Barack Obama declared that "slamming the door in the face of refugees would betray our deepest values." UK Prime

Minister David Cameron pledged to settle twenty thousand Syrian refugees.

The Syrian refugee crisis became a central election issue in Canada. Justin Trudeau, leader of the opposition Liberal Party, promised to settle twenty-five thousand Syrians in Canada by Christmas if Canadians voted for him. Harper stuck to ten thousand and promised to help chase the Islamic State out of Syria so people could return home.

Tareq wondered if they'd made a terrible mistake when they turned down the opportunity to go to France.

"It's coming. They will not forget us. We will be in Canada," his mother insisted. Her words became a family mantra: we will be in Canada. But Tareq, uncharacteristically, began to lose hope. He stopped paying attention to the news. He poured himself into his volunteer work. He was preparing for another field trip one October when his phone rang. He wrestled it out of his pocket. A private number was calling, and his battery was down to just 1 per cent. Reluctantly, he answered.

"Tareq! You are the first call that we made. Congratulations!"

Canadians had overwhelmingly voted for Trudeau, and the embassy in Beirut was working day and night to send twenty-five thousand Syrians to Canada before Christmas. The official promised to give Tareq two weeks' notice before the flight left but told him to pack his bags now. Tareq plugged in his phone and shared the news with his family. After the earlier promises and the months of waiting, part of him still didn't believe it would happen. The road diverged in front of him: one way led to safety and a new life in Canada; the other was a dead end in Lebanon.

It was a daunting, ambitious plan. How would Canadian officials get UN referrals so quickly? How would they process them? How would they get everyone to Canada? They could treat it as a humanitarian evacuation, like the one that got people out of Ivory Coast in

2004 during unrest in the West African country. That would mean putting planes on the ground, doing very basic screenings, then getting people to Canada and doing the rest of the processing once they arrived. Another option was to do the full processing abroad, so everyone on board would land with all their paperwork ready. A third, wilder option was to rent cruise ships and process people on board as they crossed the Atlantic Ocean.

The government rented a section of a Beirut hotel and filled it with extra staff to process applications. Trudeau opted for a mix of the first and second options, doing much of the processing overseas, flying Syrian refugees to Canada, and then completing the processing in Canada. Some would come as government-sponsored refugees while others were privately sponsored or a mix of the two.

Finding candidates proved harder than expected. On Canada's behalf, the UNHCR texted seventy thousand Syrians to ask if they were interested in moving to Canada. It's not known how many of those messages went to dead phones or wrong numbers. But many of those who got the message balked at the prospect of leaving everything and everyone they knew behind on just ten days' notice. Still, sixteen thousand said yes.

For most, it would be a leap into the unknown. The 2011 Canadian census showed that only about forty-one thousand Syrians or Syrian-descended people lived in the nation of 34 million. That meant few Syrians knew anybody in Canada. Some candidates were illiterate in Arabic, let alone English, and were understandably reluctant to take on the enormous challenge of starting over in such an alien country. About 9 per cent of the applicants dropped out during the vetting process. Some families made it all the way to the airport but got cold feet and wouldn't board the plane. Faced with abandoning family, including elderly and sick grandmothers, fathers, aunts, and uncles, many people decided to face death alongside them. Moving to Canada essentially meant passing through a one-way door.

During the interview stage, specially trained Canadian officials asked questions designed to spot any terrorists, former government soldiers, rebels, and others who had perpetrated the war. Five layers of security screening kept these false refugees out of Canada. At the Beirut hotel, Canadians turned one room into a classroom teaching a crash course on life in the true north strong and free. Syrians took the class to learn about Canadian culture, weather, and how they could best find a way to succeed.

In the first one hundred days, 26,172 Syrians arrived in Canada. They went to 350 communities across the country.

The embassy became a second home for the Hadhads as they returned again and again throughout November for medical tests and paperwork. Tareq learned he had his own refugee file, meaning he would be treated as an individual, while his mother and siblings remained on Isam's family file. Alaa's situation was more complicated. She and her children had entered Lebanon as tourists and had not yet been recognized as refugees. UN officials established a separate file for them and promised to figure something out. But she would likely have to stay behind as the rest of the family moved to Canada.

The Canadians told Tareq that he would go first and his family would follow. They'd come on a blended visa, meaning the federal government would support them for the first six months and private sponsors would cover the next six months. Those sponsors would also be responsible for helping the newcomers settle into their new homes. It never occurred to the Hadhads to ask where in Canada those sponsors were.

December came, and the Hadhads felt a familiar despair return. Tareq went back to volunteering. He was shuffling down the hall under a mountain of paperwork, thinking about the clinic's upcoming trip, when he got the call telling him his flight to Canada was leaving the very next day.

Jubilant, Tareq tossed the papers into the air. "Guys, I'm flying!" he exclaimed to his colleagues.

"You mean the files are flying?" one asked with a laugh.

"No!" Tareq said. "I'm flying tomorrow!" The significance of what had just happened hit him: he was really going this time. He wept and laughed. It seemed to him that the world started spinning again for the first time since he and his family fled Syria nearly three years earlier. But his face suddenly darkened. *The dialysis machine*, he thought. He had been leading an effort to get a UN grant to buy a machine to treat refugees whose kidneys had stopped working. It was supposed to arrive soon, and he was in charge of delivering it. His colleagues told him to go to Canada: they would take care of it. He insisted he would see it through, no matter where he was.

He called his family and raced home to pack his bags. He would later describe his last night in Lebanon as the best night of his life, despite the fear and anxiety. His entire family crowded together. Tareq was wild with excitement. He Googled everything he could think of about Canada and shared every detail with his sisters, brother, and parents.

On the surface, he showed enthusiasm and courage. Underneath he was terrified. His parents tried to slip away to sleep, but he insisted everyone keep vigil with him through the night. He wanted to talk. Talking calmed him down. In his head, he kept repeating to himself: your family will follow you; your family will follow you. But what if his family didn't follow him? He knew of people like him who had gone ahead to Brazil and the United States and were stranded alone when the rest of the family could not make it. Was this his family's exciting first step toward Canada, or was it the last time he'd ever be with them?

In the middle hours of the night, his sisters and brother drifted off to sleep. So did his mother and father. Tareq alone stayed awake. He thought back to the ten-storey home in Damascus, his happy childhood when the world seemed safe. He recalled the terrible days of the war, the destruction of the home, and the long flight to Lebanon.

He thought ahead to Canada, too, building houses and then tearing them down in his mind. He imagined first an igloo in the far north, where he would learn to fight polar bears, then a wood house on the west coast, where he would fend off grizzlies. Perhaps he'd make it to a big city and build a new urban life? Then he dissolved that dream and imagined himself settling into a medical practice in rural Ontario. He included his family in all of these images. He'd rather be with them in a war zone than alone somewhere else.

The whole family accompanied Tareq to his last interviews, held in the Beirut hotel. He learned that he would fly to Toronto before settling in another community where his private sponsors awaited him. His parents and siblings would follow. The official said the Hadhads could then move anywhere in Canada if they wanted to, including the big immigrant cities of Montreal, Toronto, and Vancouver.

"You are not a tree," he said. "You guys don't have roots; you have legs."

It was time to say goodbye. Isam wanted to accompany his son to the airport and hailed a taxi. Tareq hugged his sisters and brother deeply.

Batoul was excited for Tareq. He spoke to her: "I will not say goodbye, because I will see you soon. The Canadian embassy told me you will come after me."

"I hope you have a great future there," Batoul said. She heard the negative note in her words and quickly added, "I hope to see you soon, after a few years."

He smiled. "You are coming soon."

Shahnaz squeezed her towering son, wiping back tears.

Tareq put on a big smile to comfort his mother, sisters, and brother and waved goodbye. Despite his reassurances, a fearful part of him thought that he was seeing them for the last time.

Isam worried deeply for his son. Most families they knew had left as one, yet Tareq would go alone. What if the rest of the family wasn't allowed to follow? This taxi ride might be the last forty minutes he'd have with his eldest son. When he was roughly Tareq's age, Isam realized, he had decided to set out on his own path, one that led to a successful chocolate business, marriage, and happiness. He hoped Tareq would find equally good days ahead.

Father and son spoke warmly about Syria and all the good times they'd shared. They also talked about their losses: Alaa's husband, Mamdouh; their cousins Bassam and Hanan; the family home; the chocolate factory.

Isam shared what he had learned about living on your own. "Take care of yourself," he said. "I know you will do great stuff in Canada. You will travel, and I will be happy for you, and proud of you, whatever you do there." A moment of silence lapsed as Lebanon rolled by outside the car windows. Isam spoke again. "Whenever you become a Canadian citizen, visit us." Tareq, reeling at the realization that his father did not expect that any of them would join him in Canada, could not speak. Their talk turned to God and the good things of the world as the taxi approached the airport. "Canada is a big country. A big future awaits you," Isam predicted. Tareq thought of Natalie Jewett, Oscar Jacobs, and the many other Canadians in Lebanon who had worked so hard to help him and his family. Surely, he thought, only good things could happen in a nation with so many kind, loving people.

Tareq pictured his family reunited in Canada, his children and grandchildren growing up safe. He saw himself as an old man, describing how the Hadhad family escaped death in Syria for a new life in Canada. Then he saw himself alone, a man with no family and no country, no past and no future. He turned to his father.

"You will become Canadian even before me," Tareq promised, his eyes shining with tears. "You will follow me and our family will be fine. I will settle in and prepare everything for your arrival: a nice house and a good community. We lost our family of sixty. I promise you I will build a family of six hundred in Canada. When you arrive, you will feel at home."

The taxi arrived. Isam embraced his eldest son. As Isam watched Tareq walk away, he felt all his fears vanish and his heart fill with hope.

Part Two

Five

In the deep past, thick ice covered the northern lands and bitter winds howled over a world without life. Twenty thousand years ago, the world warmed and the glaciers melted, drop by drop, scraping the bedrock, sculpting smooth, low drumlins, and stranding erratic boulders as the ice retreated to its Arctic stronghold.

The first people travelled by foot and by water, advancing the ancient expansion out of Africa, across Asia, over the now-vanished Bering Strait land bridge and into the newly born lands south of their beachhead in Beringia. Humanity's great encirclement of the globe was completed fourteen thousand years ago, when the vanguard reached a lobster-shaped land clinging to the continent's east coast. L'Nuk, the People, called the land Mi'kma'ki.

L'Nuk crafted fluted tools, gravers, and spear tips to hunt the powerful caribou that migrated through their land. They gathered seafood from the ocean. Millennia passed, and Mi'kma'ki warmed again. Green forests covered the eastern peninsula. Fish entered the streams and L'Nuk began to build lives around the land's forty-four river systems. Family groups of a few dozen people lived in villages along the rivers, moving up and down the waterways with the seasons. They put down their spears and invented arrows to better hunt moose and caribou. They built weirs across the rivers to catch fish. One community settled in the northeast, in a place they called Articougnesche, or the Meeting Place of Five Forked Rivers.

Their first encounters with the pale people from across the ocean came just five hundred years ago and were friendly enough for L'Nuk to call the Europeans *ni'kaq*, my kin friends. The Europeans misunderstood and began using the name Mi'kmaq to describe L'Nuk. The Europeans first came to fish. In 1604, a French explorer named Champlain came and befriended the great Mi'kmaw leader Grand Chief Membertou.

The two peoples lived together for 150 years in Mi'kma'ki and Acadia until the British decided the land of many people must become the land of one people, the British, and tried to drive the Mi'kmaq and Acadians off the land. The violence that followed obliterated much of the ancient history.

❖

Local legend says it started as a footpath to get from Brown's Mountain to William's Point. The footpath grew into a bridle path for horse travel then a cart road that could accommodate wagons. People got tired on the twelve-mile trek and some built houses along it; others opened businesses. Eventually, they raised a church and realized they had a village. The Mi'kmaw name Articougnesche turned into Antigonish. The old footpath was grandly renamed Main Street, and the town sprung up around it. Today, elegant brick buildings populate Main Street, which branches into leafy residential roads of cozy wood homes.

Antigonish sits in northeastern Nova Scotia, about 160 kilometres from Halifax, a few kilometres inland from the Northumberland Strait that separates Nova Scotia and New Brunswick from Prince Edward Island. Unusually for Nova Scotia, where you're never more than a long walk from the coast, you can't see the water from the town. It's the lush trees that you notice, breaking through as tiny forests anywhere the people have not built houses or businesses.

A few thousand people live in Antigonish all year, but each September the population doubles when students arrive at St. Francis Xavier University, founded in 1853. Each summer, the town holds the Highland Games, created in 1863 as an athletic and cultural celebration of the Highland Scots, who were forced off their land in the 1770s and settled in Antigonish. The early settlers shared a devout Catholicism that earned the town the nickname Little Vatican. The bishop of Antigonish automatically became the chancellor of the university, a custom that would last until the twenty-first century. The Great War broke the quiet peace. Men like farmer Ronald William McDonald, born in 1894 in Malignant Cove, a coastal community just outside the town proper, eagerly signed up for the promised adventure. McDonald's family came from Scotland, so he answered the homeland's call for help. His first fighting came in the trenches of France. In April 1917, he was one of the brave Canadians to capture Vimy Ridge. He fought through Passchendaele, taking a bullet to his right thigh. He fought on, to the end of the war, and at twenty-four felt a great relief as he prepared to return to his Antigonish farm. But in England he developed a cough. Tuberculosis waged a new war inside his body. He died at the end of August 1919, becoming the town's last casualty of war. Heartbroken, Antigonish built a cenotaph on Main Street and carved McDonald's name on it, alongside more than eighty other young men who died in arms.

After the Great War, flapper dresses, jazz music, and automobiles signalled the dawn of a new era of optimism and consumerism. But not in Nova Scotia. Instead, the Roaring Twenties brought poverty as a generation of young men were not there to pick up the work of their fathers. In 1929, the stock market crashed, bringing the Great Depression to the rest of the western world. People looked for a saviour to rescue them.

On September 8, 1930, Father Moses Coady walked into a meeting in Antigonish's town hall. The Catholic priest was in his fifties; he stood six feet tall and weighed 220 pounds. He had the square face of a boxer who had won more fights than he'd lost. With his black clothes and white dog collar, he commanded respect. Coady recognized how a major economic depression would affect an already struggling place like Antigonish, and he was determined to do something about it.

At the raucous meeting, he argued with government workers, farmers, and fishermen about how to get a better life. He spoke bluntly, but he was never condescending. "The people can do ten times what they think they can do!" he insisted. "You're poor enough to want it, and smart enough to get it."

Coady proposed the working people form study clubs and use their brains to attack the problems that made life miserable. They'd lay out a plan and implement it cooperatively. Consumers would use their power to support good businesses and starve bad ones. Then Coady went out on the road to spread his message. In a ten-month period in one year in the 1930s, Coady visited every fishing village in Nova Scotia, Prince Edward Island, and New Brunswick.

When he travelled, Coady stayed with people in their homes. He listened to them. He heard what his biographer, Jim Lotz, calls a "weird pessimism" that so benumbed everybody that it seemed as though nothing could break the spell. The "country buck with the brains of a genius," as Lotz puts it in *The Humble Giant*, told the men about his rugged childhood as the son of immigrants and refugees who made the most of their new chance at life. Literacy was the key, Coady argued: if people learned to read and write, they'd have the tools to think of ways to lift themselves out of poverty. He told them they'd been robbed of their individualism. The industrialized world stole their chances for self-expression and personal initiative. They must roll a huge stone up a steep hill, he said, and they could never falter, for that would send the stone crashing back to the bottom.

Coady would stand on the beaches and the docks, next to overturned fishing boats, preaching his secular gospel to skeptical Nova Scotian fishermen. They wore tattered clothes stained with sweat and fish guts. Baggy flat caps kept the worst of the sun off. Grizzled old men wearing ancient overalls watched Coady closely before turning their eyes to the ground. These men left their homes before the sun rose. They picked through the cupboards looking for food, found only a few pieces of bread, thought about their children and their wives, and put the bread back. They rowed to sea with empty stomachs and empty nets. They sold what they caught to big companies that processed the fish and sent them to market. The companies thought they owned the fishermen, and many of the fishermen felt the same way. They lived in homes owned by the companies, they shopped in company stores, running up debts that they could never repay. If you spoke against the company, you risked losing not just your livelihood but your home. Cape Breton coal miners had recently stood up for themselves, and the coal companies kicked them out of their company-owned houses. The miners and their families lived in tents that winter.

But they had no one but themselves to blame for their poverty, Coady told them. "We have to get over the naïve idea that monop- olistic exploiters and dictators are going to reform because good men preaching justice and charity tell them to do so. We must add force to our persuasion," Coady said. "This does not mean physical force and bloodshed, but the force of ideas."

When a heckler interrupted Coady, he was quick to respond. "Listen to this stupid fellow!" Coady retorted. "He was probably given a plug of tobacco to interrupt me by asking questions that could only come from a braying ass!"

Neither the government nor the church would help them, Coady said. It was up to them. "Are we so terrified by men like ourselves that we do crouch and cower at the feet of the men we have made our masters?" Coady asked, eyes boring through each fisherman. "If we have the power to make, then we still have the power to unmake." If they were slaves, Coady said, they'd better set themselves and their whole society free. "The coal miner comes out of the pit, cleans up at the washhouse, and calls it a day. The fisherman thinks he has done enough when he lands his catch on the wharf. The farmer puts in a day of drudgery and knocks off until tomorrow. This is their great mistake. There is no standing still, and if the people do not take the means to advance themselves, they will surely slip backward." The priest rose to the mountaintop of his speech. Punching his own hard hand, he declared in a firm, loud voice: "You can do it. Do it!"

"Man, he would just lift us," one fisherman who heard Coady speak would later say. "He was a dynamic conqueror. Once you heard him, you weren't the same again."

St. Francis Xavier University gave him an office. He recruited women, a novel idea at the time. Sister Irene Doyle worked closely with him and became a key ally in promoting the Antigonish Movement. "It was a wonderful experience," she recalled in later years. "We knew we were involved in something greater than ourselves, and that was a source of great satisfaction."

Moses Coady climbed hills and descended into valleys to spread his message. He started with mass meetings to light a fire in people's hearts. He told them they were stupid and lazy to waste evenings staring at the fire in exhaustion, just to go back to the same grind the next day. He called these meetings his "intellectual bombing" operations. Over and over, he repeated his philosophy: "You can get the good life. You're poor enough to want it and smart enough to get it."

For a priest, Coady had an unusually strong appreciation of entrepreneurs. He understood that poor people looked at big companies and thought they must have been built by geniuses. Coady loved to trace business stories back to their roots and show "the origin of the whole puzzling system to have been in a one-room shack with a few rude shelves and a proprietor with a little more cunning and foresight than his fellows." He urged newly prosperous people to not forget those still in hard times. "If we are wise, we will help people everywhere to get the good and abundant life. We are all our brother's keeper, and we had better be, for one day he will be our keeper. And he may be a pretty rough keeper."

The Antigonish Movement spread across Canada and into the United States. In the late 1930s, the cardinal who would soon become Pope Pius XII praised the Antigonish Movement. "Social life has a sacredness of its own when imbued with the spirit of the gospel and based on charity and justice," Eugenio Maria Giuseppe Giovanni Pacelli wrote. In 1939, St. Francis Xavier University hosted an Antigonish Movement gathering. It attracted people from across Canada and from twenty-eight US states. The *New York Times* and the London *Times* ran major articles on the movement. "How many of the educated and intelligent people who read this supplement have ever heard of Antigonish?" the British reporter asked. "Yet amid the multitude of crowded experience, nothing moved me so much as the work of...Antigonish."

More than a dozen men of Antigonish lost their lives in World War II. Their names were carved on the cenotaph. But good times followed. In the 1950s, the smell of asphalt filled the town as it became the first in the province to pave all its streets. The yearly influx of university students brought new life to the town, and in 1957, St. Francis Xavier's winning football team was dubbed the "Assassins from Antigonish" in a profile in *Time* magazine. Many of the young people studied with Moses Coady and then took his message to Africa, South America, and Asia. "It doesn't give us only dollars and cents," one member said. "It teaches us to trust one another, to transact business with one another, and best of all it teaches us to live in peace and harmony with one another."

Coady was in the midst of a speech when he collapsed on stage in 1958. He died the following summer, at age seventy-seven, at his home in Antigonish. Some of the seeds he sowed fell on rocky ground, and others among thorns. But many fell into good soil. A few months after his death, St. Francis Xavier University opened the Coady International Institute to teach the world how to use cooperation and consumerism to lift people out of poverty.

Coady published his only book, *Masters of Their Own Destiny*, in 1939. Seeing the dark clouds of war looming on the horizon, Coady wrote words that could have been spray-painted on a Syrian wall decades later. People "were not born to hate but to love . . . and we are the victims of a vicious system bred by greed and nurtured by the will to power," Coady declared. "Man was not made for bestial fighting. Man was conceived in peace. And in peace he shall find his lost virtues and his departed joys."

❖

Lucille Harper turned off the news about the war in Syria and decided it was time to act.

It was spring 2015, and the Islamic State was on the rise. Millions of mothers and fathers, sons and daughters, sisters and brothers were fleeing the chaos. Lucille was not related to Canada's prime minister, Stephen Harper, but she often joked she wished she was his older sister so she could grab him by the ear. His government saw Syria as a military problem and had pledged another $360 million to fight the Islamic State in the Middle East. The prime minister argued that airlifting thousands of refugees from Syria and Iraq could put Canadians at risk, as Islamic terrorists could use that as cover to enter the country. Critics like federal NDP leader Tom Mulcair accused Harper of using that as an excuse to turn his back on the refugee crisis.

In the United States, presidential candidate Donald Trump called the Syrian refugees an army and said he'd send them all home if he won the 2016 election. One million asylum seekers entered Germany, straining public resources and sparking social tension. As the cities reached capacity, the government sent refugees to villages. In Freital, near Dresden, refugees hid inside a hotel as locals yelled from the streets and threatened to burn the place down.

Lucille had watched news story after news story about families that drowned as they tried to cross the Mediterranean. She wanted to do something, but what could one woman in Antigonish achieve on her own? She needed a group.

We can't solve the situation in Syria, we can't solve the refugee crisis, but we can rescue one grain of sand on the beach, Lucille thought. *We'll try to bring a refugee family here and we'll do the best job that we can.*

Lucille went to her computer and opened her email program. She entered the addresses of fourteen people she thought might be willing and able to join her. She typed "Syrian refugee family" into the subject line. "I've been thinking a lot about what has been happening in Syria, Canada's role in the Middle East, and whether we might be able as a community to support a refugee family," she wrote. She asked her friends if they'd like to get together in person to talk about what they could do. "I know this will not be something everyone will want to participate in, so no pressure — just seeing who might like to be involved," she wrote. She signed her name and pressed send.

Heather Mayhew was in her airy kitchen when she read Lucille's email. She'd been watching the Syrian war, too, and wanted to help. Both her sons were grown. One was studying to be a doctor, and the other was travelling the world. Her youngest child, her daughter Carly, was the last one at home, and she would be leaving soon, hopefully to attend university in Halifax.

Heather liked to remind people her name came from the resilient flowering plant that thrives on wind-swept coasts. She and her husband, Frank Gallant, both worked at Peak Experiences Consulting, a company Frank had founded in Antigonish in 1992. They helped companies, governments, and other organizations to look at problems from fresh perspectives and improve. She brought decades of experience working in ecology, teaching, and activism to her role.

A few years earlier, Heather and Frank had paid off the mortgage on their home. They decided to keep the payment in their budget and purchase a second house. Heather was a long-time volunteer with the Antigonish Poverty Reduction Coalition and knew the village desperately needed affordable housing. She and Frank bought and repaired a two-storey yellow house situated on a major road just a short walk from the village centre and rented it out to a family at a low rate. That family had recently left Antigonish, and she and Frank were seeking a new family in need. Maybe the Syrian family could use the home. She told Lucille to count her in.

Two weeks later, on May 5, all fourteen people who had received Lucille's email sat in a circle of comfy chairs by the sunny window overlooking Main Street at the Antigonish Women's Resource Centre. They were joined by three others who had heard about Lucille's idea. The group was growing before it even started. All of its members lived in Antigonish, and everyone knew Lucille, but little else tied them together.

Lucille opened the meeting by bluntly laying out the enormous challenge ahead of them. If they wanted to sponsor one family of six people, they'd first have to raise between $32,000 and $52,000.

Five members of the group would have to sign documents swearing to assist the refugee family; those same five people would also have to pledge to donate money to them. The federal government would provide some funding, but the group would have to find the family housing, furniture, and clothing. They would have to get the children enrolled in school. The group would have to fill in reams of forms and prepare the community for the new family, and it could be three years before the family arrived. Even after three years of hard work, it might not happen at all. And even if everything worked out, the family would be under no obligation to stay in Antigonish.

Bronwen Cooke volunteered immediately. She knew little about the Syrian war and had three young children. Her days were packed, but she knew she would find time. Helping was the right thing to do, so she'd do it.

"Could we identify a family through Syrian-Canadians already living here?" one member asked, but nobody could think of a single Syrian in Antigonish County. Sheila Sears, who worked as the director of public health for the Guysborough Antigonish Strait Health Authority, said she knew a Syrian family in nearby Guysborough County. She offered to ask them for ideas.

Rennae Kletzel-Gilham, a friend of Bronwen who had recently moved her young family from Alberta to Nova Scotia, said she'd talk to a friend at the World University Service of Canada to see if they could sponsor people through its programs. Some offered to talk to the local United Church to see if they wanted to help. Others offered to contact the Anglicans and Catholics and a group in nearby Inverness about their experience getting a family from Sierra Leone to Nova Scotia. The group decided it needed a name and quickly settled on Syria–Antigonish Families Embrace, or SAFE.

Heather left feeling a bit shocked at the amount of work it would take to rescue one family. But she knew Lucille well. Lucille was a diplomatic, determined person who found ways to get things done. Her energy could carry the group forward. Lucille indeed felt encouraged. Her group had accepted the challenge calmly and its members were smart enough to make it happen. But, mindful of Lucille's warnings, everyone left the meeting expecting that it could be a long time until they were able to get a family to Canada.

SAFE began its preliminary work. They set up a booth at the local farmers' market to let people know of their project and sign up more volunteers. Then September came, and the photographs of Alan Kurdi's body turned Lucille's metaphorical grain of sand into flesh and blood. SAFE shared the photo and urged people to take selfies holding signs saying #Refugeeswelcome. Dozens of locals responded to the challenge, and more stopped by SAFE's booth at the farmers' market. In the days after Alan Kurdi's death, SAFE grew from fifteen members to more than one hundred. Five days later, they'd raised $10,000, the minimum sum they needed to identify an eligible family and bring them to Canada.

A few weeks later, just four months after SAFE's first meeting, they passed their three-year fundraising goal. They could help a second family. When Justin Trudeau's Liberal Party won the October federal election and pledged to bring twenty-five thousand Syrians to Canada by Christmas, SAFE went into warp speed.

SAFE applied to bring the families to Canada under the Blended Visa Office-Referred Program, which matched refugees with private sponsors. The federal government would provide funds for the first six months, and the private group would be on the hook for the second six months. The government provided SAFE with a long list of families to choose from, but only identified them by age and gender—no names or occupations. SAFE ruled out families with serious or complex medical needs that would be better served in a large city, and they looked for large families, so they could help as many people as possible.

The village embraced the project. Annie Chau's family had come to Canada from Vietnam in 1979, part of the boat people refugees. Canada had embraced them, and now she wanted to pay it forward. So did Robert Sers, a retired surgeon, whose Latvian father had immigrated to Canada after World War II. Sers and his wife, Moira, a judge, were happy to join SAFE. The group's clear-eyed, pragmatic approach impressed them both. More than two hundred people gave money, donated sheets and clothing, volunteered to paint walls and clean floors, or offered to serve as drivers and tutors for the families. Some even offered to learn how to cook Syrian food and then stock the homes with familiar ingredients. Others gave toys for the children. Asana Yoga, which operated in a space on Main Street, started holding Friday Karma Classes. The classes were free, but they collected donations for SAFE. The Antigonish International Film Festival screened a documentary about the Syrian conflict and donated proceeds to SAFE. The Antigonish Holistic Wellness and Psychic Fair donated all of its admission fees to SAFE.

Heather put in long hours on SAFE's education committee, which would help the Syrian children enrol in the local school. They figured out the logistics of continuing a Syrian education in Canada and gathered potential mentors and tutors to help the Syrian children learn English as they studied. She and Lucille observed that preparing to welcome the Syrian families built a new community in Antigonish. People who had been strangers to one another before worked side by side and formed close friendships. It was also an educational experience. Many of them were activists against poverty, but few of them had actually been poor. The Syrian families would receive only as much money as Canadians on income assistance, and the group learned just how hard it was to find housing and cover basic expenses on that sum of money.

Lucille's SAFE team decided to keep fundraising to see just how many grains of sand they could pluck from the beach. They filled the fall with information sessions and fundraising events. They held benefit concerts and pancake breakfasts. They operated the booth at the farmers' market most weekends to recruit new members.

In late October, SAFE shared on its Facebook page the news that the government had matched the group with its first family: the Hadhads. "They need to go through interviews and paperwork, so we are waiting. Could be within weeks or months!"

SAFE knew only their names. They had no photos, no biographies, no clue what the family had done in Syria, nor what they hoped to do in Canada. The Hadhads would live in Heather Mayhew and Frank Gallant's yellow rental house. SAFE began looking for a home for the second family. They hoped to find one within walking distance of the village centre, hospital, and schools.

When SAFE gathered for their monthly meetings in the women's centre or the public library, they often talked about the culture shock the families would go through in moving from a culturally Muslim Middle Eastern city to a culturally Christian North American village. They contacted CBC reporter Natasha Fatah, who told them about her experiences in Syria, and her encounters with anti-Muslim sentiment. At another meeting, they listened to Ghandi Mohrez talk about his immigration experience. Ghandi had been a mechanical engineer in Syria. In 2000, after the death of President Hafez al-Assad, he and his new wife, Dima, decided to emigrate. Syria didn't offer enough freedom, they felt. Seeing Canadian peacekeepers at work inspired Ghandi to learn about Canada.

His first job was serving pizza to drunk Haligonians on the city's celebrated Pizza Corner, an intersection named for the pizzerias on three of its four corners (a Presbyterian church occupies the fourth). Ghandi later bought Big G's Pizza in rural Guysborough, where he employed three people full-time, year-round, and six more during the summer.

Ghandi and Dima's two children, nearly adults, knew no other home than Nova Scotia. But he knew most immigrants would not stay in a rural area. Jobs were scarce and opportunities were limited. "When you give, you can't have expectations as to what the result will be," he told the SAFE group. "They may stay, and they may decide they have to leave. And then you've put all this effort in, and they may need to go to Toronto or Montreal."

Ghandi also recorded a video teaching some basic Arabic phrases so the Nova Scotians could greet the newcomers in their own language.

As November turned into December, SAFE learned more details about the Hadhads. The eldest son was twenty-three and would arrive first. His parents and younger siblings would follow on a family visa.

Heather visited the yellow house to make sure it was ready. The closets were stocked with donated towels, linens, and bedding. Dishes and food filled the kitchen cupboards. She and Frank had replaced the old house's windows, and light suffused the rooms.

"It's so beautiful and welcoming," she marvelled.

They'd also installed fitted blinds in each window. For Muslims, a home has to be a fully private place. The Hadhad women could wear indoor clothing only when they were with their family or with other women. If a man from outside the family came to the home, they would go to their rooms and dress in their modest outdoor clothing. Having clear windows that anybody could look through would be like having a strange man visiting all the time.

And then, on the last Saturday before Christmas, just eight months after Lucille Harper sent her email, a convoy of around twenty people left Antigonish. They drove for two hours under cloudy skies on a sub-zero day, arriving at the airport in Halifax well before Tareq Hadhad's flight was due. A Yarmouth group was

also there to welcome its own family of refugees, and the two groups
chatted as they waited for the Syrians to arrive.

Bronwen wondered how they'd recognize him. They had no clue
what he looked like. Her excitement mixed with sorrow. She thought
about how sad she would be if she had to flee her homeland, and how
scared she'd feel arriving as a stranger in a strange land.

Lucille stood near the foot of the stairs holding a welcome sign.
She'd brought an interpreter. She didn't know how much English
Tareq spoke, and she figured the long trip would exhaust him,
anyway. At least they could speak to him in his own language and
explain to him why they were about to drive deep into the woods
of northern Nova Scotia.

Passengers began descending the stairs. Lucille kept watch for a
lone man who looked like he might have just fled the Middle East.
A handsome man coming down the stairs with the confident air
of an arriving celebrity caught her attention. He was tall—six feet
three inches—and wore a black winter coat trimmed in fake fur,
blue jeans, and a tidy beard. Was this Tareq Hadhad? And if it was,
why was he carrying a baby?

Six

When the chartered plane left the tarmac in Beirut, bound for Amman, Jordan, it was the first time Tareq had ever been airborne. A few hours later, he boarded his second flight and looked out the window as the plane flew over the Mediterranean Sea and headed for the Atlantic Ocean.

He shifted excitedly in his seat, his mind buzzing, imagining the possibilities that lay ahead of him. He could finally finish his medical studies and become a physician; he could get a humanitarian job with an NGO; maybe he could become something entirely new. He also thought of the family he'd left behind. When he looked out the rounded window, he saw their anxious eyes.

Looking around the plane's interior, he spotted a Syrian man a few rows ahead of him. The man seemed to radiate anxiety. When it was safe to unbuckle his seatbelt, Tareq bent his tall frame and went up the aisle to talk to the man. Like Tareq, he was bound for resettlement in Canada. He could speak neither English nor French, and he didn't know anybody in Canada. He had no cellphone and so he was cut off from the people he'd left behind.

"*Ana khayif*," the man said in Arabic: I am afraid. "I see myself stuck in a situation where I can't communicate and I'm lost."

Tareq crouched beside him and smiled encouragingly. He took out his phone and offered it to the man, telling him that he could find tutorials on YouTube that would help him learn a few English phrases. The man accepted eagerly and was soon repeating in English, "It's beautiful weather out there. It's beautiful weather out there." Tareq returned to his seat.

Tareq smiled as he folded himself back into his seat. He adjusted his long legs so they wouldn't cause discomfort to the passenger in the seat ahead of him. *If you want to receive kindness, you must give kindness*, he thought.

Tareq had no idea where he was going after he landed in Toronto. As the airplane banked over snowy Labrador, his mind replayed a conversation he'd had with a Canadian official in Lebanon.

"Where do you want to stay?" the official had asked.

Tareq had done his research. "MTV," he replied. The official laughed. Tareq clarified: "Montreal, Toronto, or Vancouver." He figured his family, used to living in a big city, would do best in an urban setting. But the official cautioned him. He thought a small town would offer the Hadhads the best chance of building new lives, because there they would be more likely to be welcomed into the community. In one of the large cities, no one would notice them, care about them, or feel a responsibility to help them.

Tareq found the idea intriguing.

The airplane approached Toronto Pearson International Airport. With a whir and a bump, the landing gear deployed, and the aircraft bounced on the runway, decelerating to a stop. The pilot's voice crackled onto the speakers, welcoming passengers to an overcast, chilly December 18, 2015. Tareq let the front of the plane disembark before he stood and stretched in the aisle.

His phone rang as soon as it connected to the internet. "Toronto now!" his mother exclaimed. "How does it feel, my Neil Armstrong?" It was late at night in Lebanon, but Shahnaz had been calling her son every hour while he was flying. Hearing his voice after he landed safely in Canada felt to Shahnaz like the moment when Viola Armstrong heard her son's voice from the moon. Shahnaz and Tareq had a quick, excited chat, and he promised to update her when he got settled. He gathered his things, bent his head, and headed for the exit. The anxious Syrian man was still repeating, "It's beautiful weather out there."

Tareq smiled encouragingly. The 214 Syrians slowly passed through customs and collected their luggage. Theirs was just the second flight bringing Syrian refugees to Canada. Tareq had only a backpack. He sensed an important figure had entered the waiting area when an older man with thinning white hair and a tidy suit smiled and said, "Marhaba" — hello. He was introduced as David Johnston, the governor general of Canada. Tareq learned that this man was the queen's representative in Canada and the formal head of state, although the elected prime minister in fact ran the country. Johnston stood with his wife, daughter, and four grandchildren. One Syrian man asked for permission to kiss the governor general and pecked him on both cheeks.

"It is an honour to be welcomed by you," the man said.

"The Canadian people welcome you very warmly," Johnston replied, beaming. The young children handed out wool toques, and other volunteers distributed winter coats. Tareq received a puffy black coat with a fur hood and quickly pulled it on to chase out the cold. Johnston went around the room, greeting the newcomers. "We are happy to have you and your family here. Your children will quickly make friends with children like our grandchildren."

None of the newcomers could have identified Johnston when they woke up that morning, but everyone understood what he represented. If the queen's representative wanted you in Canada, who could object? Johnston told a reporter he was confident this group of newcomers would soon settle into new lives, as would the thousands of people still to come. "Wave upon wave of immigrants have come and found this is a good land. We're reaching into our traditions, our history, and our most fundamental values, and that we must continue to reinforce."

He distributed copies of Canada's Charter of Rights and Freedoms to each family. Tareq got his own copy and held it like a holy relic. He noticed the governor general didn't call them Syrians or refugees. He called them new Canadians—from the moment they landed.

The new Canadians were directed to the airport hotel where they would stay for the night. An immigration official approached Tareq and the anxious Syrian man in the hotel lobby. The man opened his mouth to speak as the official reached them. Tareq realized what he was about to say too late to stop him.

"It's beautiful weather out there!" the anxious man blurted out.

The official looked at him in astonishment. "Are you serious? It's freezing cold!"

The man asked Tareq for his phone. He did some quick Googling and then corrected himself. "It's horrible weather out there!" Both Tareq and the official burst out laughing.

"Okay, you're all set," the official told Tareq. "Your flight will leave tomorrow."

"Oh. To where?" Tareq asked.

"Halifax."

"What's Halifax? I want to stay in Canada!" Tareq protested.

"Halifax is just on the other side of the country. You will find people who have been waiting for you a long time. They will be very pleased to see you," the official assured him.

After a sleepless night in the hotel, Tareq boarded his next flight and took a seat in the back row. He thought to himself, *Here's another first: first commercial flight.* He watched three people take the seats on the opposite side of the aisle. They were Syrians, he had no doubt about that, a young man, a young woman, and a young child. He recognized the fear lurking in their eyes and smiled at the man. They exchanged greetings in Arabic.

The airplane filled with happy travellers heading home for Christmas on Canada's Celtic East Coast. Most were anticipating feasts, fiddles, and family. A voice crackled over the speakers. Tareq prepared to translate the safety instructions for his new friends, but the captain had a different announcement. "We have very special guests on board," he told the passengers. "Four refugees fleeing the Syrian war for new lives in Canada."

Someone let out a cheer near the front of the plane, and it rippled all the way to the back. Soon passengers were on their feet, clapping, cheering, and whistling for the newcomers. Tareq grinned and explained the commotion to the family. They barely seemed able to comprehend what was happening.

For years, they had lived in fear, worried that their government would kill or imprison them, that rebels would shoot them, or that they would die in a terrorist attack. They'd been made to feel that most of the world didn't want Middle Eastern Muslim refugees. And here was a plane full of Canadians whooping and hollering as if the pilot had said Sidney Crosby and Wayne Gretzky were on board with the Stanley Cup. *This is a very sweet moment*, Tareq thought.

The flight to Halifax was a turbulent one. The plane juddered up and down. The seatbelt sign stayed lit. Tareq assured the Syrian family that this was normal, hoping to himself that he was speaking the truth. None of the Canadian passengers appeared concerned, he noted. He asked for a cup of water and promptly spilled it on his lap as the plane bounced again. The family gripped their armrests. Tareq forced himself to smile. "Nothing worse than what happened in Syria could happen now," he told them. "We cannot die now; we're just in the last phase!"

The Syrians relaxed. The mother held her curly-haired toddler close. "He is going to have a better future, a better life, than I've had," she told Tareq. Tareq exchanged smiles with the boy, who seemed fresh with the promise of the newly born. Tareq felt the same way.

After two hours, the plane dropped from the sky like a star descending on the east. Tareq looked out his window and saw the dark shape of a lightless land. Halifax's airport sits far outside the city, surrounded by forests and lakes. He spotted the runway lights just before the plane bumped down. The flight attendant asked the Syrians to stay on board while the other passengers disembarked. Many looked back with friendly and encouraging smiles before they headed off the plane.

The captain walked to the back of the plane and introduced himself to the Syrians. He asked if they had any questions. They had plenty, but none for him. A flight attendant beckoned the family to follow her. Tareq was the last passenger to leave the plane. He stepped onto the gangway and felt a punch of cold air. He stared in disbelief as his phone told him it was -13°C. *For a Middle Eastern man, this is very cold,* he thought.

He quickly messaged his family in Lebanon to tell them he had landed safely in Halifax. He pulled the winter coat tight and walked to the gate. He planned to make his way into the city, probably by taxi, and find a hotel room for the night before making contact with SAFE the next day. But an Air Canada employee stopped him and said she'd call downstairs to tell them he'd arrived.

"Tell who?" he asked.

"There's a group waiting for you," she answered.

Once she'd signalled to him to proceed, Tareq strode quickly to the stairs. He found the Syrian family struggling at the top. The father was wrestling with their carry-on bags. The mother held her toddler. They both looked exhausted.

"May I carry the baby?" Tareq asked her.

The mother smiled and handed her son to Tareq. She and her husband went down the stairs first. Standing at the bottom were two groups of people beaming at them and holding signs of welcome written in English and Arabic. Tareq spotted one sign that read, "Welcome to Canada Tareq!" He assumed the sign referred to someone famous and glanced behind him to see if this celebrity Tareq was descending the stairs to greet his fans. But no one was behind him.

"Are you Tareq?" Sheila Sears asked.

"Yes, I am Tareq. But I am sure I'm not the Tareq you're looking for," he replied.

She laughed. "Yes, you are the Tareq we are looking for. And the child?"

Tareq seemed surprised to find himself still holding the boy. He laughed and returned him to his mother.

Sheila introduced him to the rest of the SAFE team. "This is Robert Sers, who will drive you home tonight, and this is Dr. Abdulrahim Alawashez, who will help translate for you."

Abdulrahim greeted Tareq and said he could call him Rahim. He was a Saudi by birth and a Canadian by choice. He was fluent in English and Arabic. He was also a colleague of Robert's, and the two doctors were delighted to help the young medical student. Tareq would stay with Robert and his wife, Moira, for a few days, until he felt ready to move into the yellow house that was awaiting him and his family.

Tareq smiled and shook each hand in turn. He fought back tears. He'd left his mother and father on the other side of the planet, but these people were welcoming him like a beloved son. It suddenly hit him: today was a very big day for these people, too.

Sheila handed him a bouquet of fresh flowers and told him they could leave soon. She saw the confusion on his face and explained that they had a two-hour drive ahead of them. "You'll enjoy it," she said. "It's trees, and it's beautiful."

Rahim mentioned that both he and Robert were surgeons. Tareq acted horrified. "But I still need my kidneys!" he joked.

As they travelled in Robert's Ford truck, Tareq told them how his family had been prosperous in Damascus before the war destroyed their business and their home. He told them about the rocket that nearly killed him and his brother. Then the talk turned to medicine, Tareq's thwarted studies, and his new dream to become a Canadian physician.

The Ford sped through the night, a comet of light leaving a trail of snow swirling in the darkness behind it. Snow-dressed trees lined the road. Few cars disturbed the peace. Tareq looked out the window. Snow fell heavily as they passed Truro, and by the time they reached New Glasgow, only a small halo of light guided them through the storm. They turned onto the Trans-Canada Highway and passed over the northern mountains. Tareq was exhausted, but he could not sleep.

"You know, fifty or sixty years ago, my father and his family were in the same situation," Robert said. "They were in a refugee camp for three and a half years." Rolf Sers, Robert's father, had been born into a happy family in Latvia. He became a physician, and on his very first day of work, in July 1940, the Soviet Union invaded. Rolf escaped persecution by working as a doctor for the Soviets. The Nazis invaded in 1941, and Rolf agreed to work as physician on the German frontline. In 1944, he fled with the Germans as the Red Army took control of Latvia again. He managed to get to England.

He learned that Canada needed doctors so he decided to relocate there. In a stroke of extraordinary good fortune, he met an Irish doctor who had just returned from studying at St. Francis Xavier University. The Irish doctor said the town needed a doctor and could not find one locally. As Rolf was preparing to leave for Nova Scotia, he fell in love with an English doctor named Phyllis. In 1950, when Rolf was thirty-five, they decided to marry and move to Nova Scotia together.

He found the people of Antigonish eager to help him. The owner of a car dealership set him up with a black two-door Chevrolet and declined to take a down payment. Rolf, he said, could pay for the car as he earned money. The drugstore gave him credit for the medical supplies he needed to set up his business. His very first case was a prominent local citizen who was thought to be dying of cancer. Rolf reached a different conclusion, prescribed antibiotics, and saved the man's life. Rolf and Phyllis told their children how lucky they were to live in Canada. Their son, Robert, followed in his father's footsteps and became a doctor in Antigonish. "Now we can help other people," he told Tareq, "and one day you will help other refugees, too."

Robert turned the Ford off the highway and into Antigonish. The main streets had been plowed, but the sidewalks were thick with snow. Lampposts shone with Christmas lights, and the houses glowed red, white, and green. Robert and Rahim pointed out the shadowy bulk of St. Francis Xavier University and the nearby Coady Institute. Tareq tried to take it in but saw only darkness.

Robert pulled into his driveway and turned off the engine. Tareq shivered as he walked up the dark driveway, stepping carefully on the snow and ice. Frozen stars sparkled through gaps in the clouds. The front door opened. Out spilled light, warmth, and the smell of cooking chicken. Moira stood in the doorway, smiling. "Come inside," she told him.

Tareq flushed with shame as he realized he had no gift to offer. He searched his mind. His eyes settled on the flowers Sheila had given him at the airport. He gently plucked a blossom and handed it to his host. Moira nodded as she accepted the gift. Her heart warmed to this young man from Damascus. His thoughtfulness astonished her. She placed the flower in a bowl of water on the table so that every time they ate, she could acknowledge his gift. She showed Tareq to his room and left him to settle in. Moira had learned how to cook a Middle Eastern meal and made a special trip to Halifax to buy the halal chicken. Robert was soon dispatched upstairs to fetch Tareq for the feast.

Tareq hesitated. "Where does the sun rise?" he asked Robert, who thought for a moment and then pointed east. Tareq thanked him and said he would be right down. He fell to his hands and knees, oriented himself to Mecca, and thanked God. "You alone do we worship and You alone do we ask for help. Lead us along the Straight Path, the path of those upon whom You have bestowed your favours," he recited in Arabic.

He felt calm as he went downstairs. The smells of spices and meat reminded him of family feasts at home. The table was set with a red tablecloth. Electric candles glowed in the windows.

Lucille sat at the head of the table and carried the burden of conversation. Rahim sat across from Tareq to help with translation. Sheila sat next to Rahim. A few other SAFE volunteers rounded out the dinner party. Tareq listened to their stories, laughed heartily at their jokes, and shared a little of his past. Sometime around midnight, he excused himself, retired to his room, and fell into a deep sleep.

❖

The next morning, dawn broke late as Antigonish approached the winter solstice. The sun cast cold rays over the pretty village. Churchgoers marched through thick snow for the fourth and final Sunday of Advent, the season awaiting the moment God entered our world. The white snow lay on the village like a thick blanket.

In the Sers home, Tareq woke early, prayed, and went downstairs, where he found Robert already up. Robert cooked Tareq a small breakfast. They spoke in low voices. Eight adult children, ranging in age from twenty-seven to forty-one, comprised Robert and Moira's blended family. Many of them were coming home for Christmas, and the big house would soon fill up. Tareq had many Christian friends in Syria and knew something of the holiday, but this would be his first time experiencing it personally. He realized it was a stroke of luck to arrive during the holidays when people were gathering with their families and friends instead of rushing off to work each day.

He looked out the window and saw it was snowing again, another thirty centimetres covering last night's big fall. Robert donned his winter armour to go shovel the driveway. "May I help?" Tareq asked. Robert was glad to teach Tareq the Canadian art of snow removal. Tareq tied on his big boots—another gift—pulled up the hood of his winter coat, and borrowed a pair of mittens.

Robert showed him the trick of pushing the big scoop full of snow and then dumping it to the side of the driveway to avoid lifting the burden. Robert snapped a photograph as Tareq gave it a try. Tareq dropped the shovel, spread his arms wide and his grin wider, and posed. The pleasure of the activity was spoiled only when Tareq learned they'd have to shovel again later that day, and likely the next day, too. It occasionally snowed in Damascus, a light dust that always melted quickly. But the Serses assured him that sometime around May, winter would end.

On Monday, Tareq stepped out of the Sers home on Church Street and followed Robert's directions to town. He compared the sleepy village to bustling, ancient Damascus. Damascus streets were narrow and jammed with small cars weaving their way through throngs of people. The awnings of the crumbling concrete buildings stretched over the streets. There were no front lawns and few trees, and there was little grass.

By contrast, the streets of Antigonish were wide and empty. Houses were surrounded by large lots filled with smooth white snow. Giant trees, bare in the winter, towered over the buildings. The vehicles were huge: big pickup trucks and SUVs. Tareq reached Main Street. One building sported a big sign in Chinese and English: Moonlight Restaurant. Next to it, a two-storey brick building housed a real estate agency and a flower shop. He turned left.

In Damascus, shops hung their merchandise outside to attract people. Children sat on the paving stones selling shirts and toys. People slowed to buy things and stopped to chat. Anytime and anywhere in Damascus, you would find crowds outside. In Antigonish, everything was inside, including most of the people. Those who did go outside climbed into their trucks and SUVs to drive even short distances, before parking again and walking quickly to their next stop.

Tareq visited the library, a pleasant building with big windows and stacks of books. He got his first Canadian library card. He went to the bank and opened an account. He pressed on, turning off Main Street to explore residential roads. People noticed him. The *Casket*, the town newspaper, had published an article about his arrival. A tall, lone Syrian man stood out in Antigonish, and Tareq found strangers extending their hands to greet him. He stopped and talked to them. Their friendliness surprised him.

One day before Christmas, Bronwen picked Tareq up. She drove him around, showing him parts of Antigonish he hadn't seen yet, and took him shopping. Tareq bought presents for the Sers family and had his first cup of Tim Hortons coffee.

Robert introduced him to the neighbours on Church Street, and Tareq met the small but growing Arabic community and joined them in Islamic worship. He met Middle Eastern professors at the university and doctors at the hospital, and they told him how they had rebuilt their lives in Nova Scotia. Some had come to the Coady Institute for a short visit, then fell in love with Antigonish and stayed. Tareq visited the university and toured the campus. He went to the arena and watched his first hockey game. He knew basketball, but hockey was new to him. The speed of play and the roughness of the checks amazed him, and the moment when the puck hit the back of the net thrilled him.

He messaged his family constantly to let them know what he was doing. He was desperate for word that they, too, were coming to Canada. In the meantime, he would gather the six hundred people he had promised his father would greet him in his new home. The first handshakes, the first hugs, the first laughs, and the first tears—these things would live with him forever. He would tell his children, and they would know how the Hadhads became Canadians.

But Robert and Moira were worried. Two nights in a row, Tareq went to his room after supper and didn't come back down. They could hear him speaking intensely in Arabic. They thought he felt reluctant to join their family gathering, and on the third evening, Robert went upstairs and knocked on Tareq's door. Tareq answered, but he was in the middle of a phone call. When he'd finished, Robert asked him if everything was okay. Tareq explained about the kidney dialysis machine he and his colleagues at the mobile medical clinic had been hoping to buy. The machine had not arrived before he'd left Lebanon, so he was spending his evenings on the phone, trying to get the job done. Robert made sure Tareq knew he was welcome to spend his evenings with the Serses if he wanted, and Tareq thanked him. The next day, he received the news he'd been waiting for: the dialysis machine had arrived and was already at work.

Tareq now turned his full attention to Christmas in Canada. The house filled with Robert's and Moira's adult children. They greeted Tareq like a brother. They also taught him how to wash the dishes and clean his clothes, new skills for a man from a world where mothers, sisters, and wives did all the housework; the one domestic task Tareq had mastered was ironing his shirts and pants. He was an eager if somewhat inept student. They also introduced him to Canadian humour via the satirical news show *This Hour Has 22 Minutes.*

On Christmas Eve, Tareq went to bed early and woke before the sun rose. After his morning prayers to Allah, he joined the Sers family downstairs. He stopped at the living room threshold and took in the scene. He had seen Christmas morning so many times in movies that he felt like he was walking onto a familiar set. Against the dark window, the Christmas tree sparkled with lights, tinsel, and glittering decorations. The strong scent of pine filled the room with an earthy warmth. The lower limbs of the tree reached protectively over a pile of presents. Santa Claus had come for everyone, including Tareq. Sipping steaming coffee, the family began to hand out the gifts.

Later that morning, when the presents were opened and everyone was fully awake, someone suggested a game of Catch Phrase, in which players are given a phrase and must get their team to guess it without saying it. Realizing Tareq was speaking a second language and in an alien culture, they cut him some slack—until he started beating them and sibling rivalry kicked in. Moira's son sat at the piano and started to play. Her daughter sang. Moira watched Tareq slip his phone out of his pocket, touch a few buttons, whisper, and then point it at the gathering. She realized he was livestreaming to his family in Lebanon, showing them the celebration, telling them to listen to the singing. He was showing them that he was safe and with good people.

Several times that day, Tareq slipped away, oriented himself to Mecca, and prayed. It was an extraordinary ordinary Canadian Christmas.

Later that night, Shahnaz asked Tareq to send her some pictures of Antigonish. She, too, had expected the family would settle in Toronto and was quickly catching up on Canadian geography. You could drive across Syria in a single day. It would take two weeks to cross Canada. Tareq looked at the photo Robert had taken of him shovelling snow and remembered his family's horrified reaction at the thought of moving to a cold country. His mother had once been able to reach out her bedroom window to pick an apricot off the tree. He searched Google for pictures of Antigonish in the summer and sent his mother a collection of bright sunny days, with green fields bursting into colourful flowers and everyone wearing summer clothing.

"Oh, it's a beautiful town. Very green," Shahnaz said approvingly.

He figured he'd tell her about winter later.

On Boxing Day, Tareq was invited to play street hockey. He casually scored a hat trick, to everyone's delight. He bought his first Canadian phone and inserted the SIM card. An hour later, before he'd given the number to anyone, his phone rang. When he answered, a woman with a strong accent addressed him as Catherine.

"Sorry, ma'am," Tareq said. "I couldn't really understand what you are saying. It's a pretty heavy accent for me."

"Who is this?" the woman asked. She was trying to reach her daughter, who had previously had that phone number. Tareq explained that he'd just acquired the number, and they ended up chatting. The woman was from Newfoundland, which accounted for her accent, but had recently moved to Nova Scotia. Her daughter had just left Nova Scotia to return to Newfoundland. Tareq told her that he was a Syrian newcomer living in Antigonish.

"I'm in the Annapolis Valley! How's the weather up there?" she asked.

They talked for thirty minutes. Tareq learned the etiquette of an East Coast phone call: you spend fifteen minutes saying hello, one minute on the purpose of the call, and fifteen minutes saying goodbye. Even if it's a wrong number.

The woman from Newfoundland called him again the next week. This time her husband joined the call. They called Tareq again the next week, and the week after that. The number that had once belonged to her daughter was now the number of her new Syrian friend, and she checked in on him until he was settled. *This country certainly has something very sweet to offer the world,* he thought. *What sweetness can I offer in return?*

Eleven days after his arrival in Canada, Tareq prepared to do his first television interview. CBC Nova Scotia wanted to find a Syrian family to follow during their first year in Canada. The story of the coming refugees had dominated the fall news, and CBC wanted a realistic portrait of a family, scarred by war, adapting to a new—perhaps hostile—country. Reporter Carolyn Ray, who had done a story about Lucille Harper in the fall, drove through a blizzard to reach Antigonish. The drive that should have taken two hours took three, and she apologized when she finally arrived, brushing the snow from her hair. Because the newsroom ran with a skeleton crew during the holidays, Carolyn came alone. She would not only interview Tareq but would shoot the story, too. Robert and Moira had worried that Tareq could be tricked into misspeaking or hounded into reliving trauma, and they planned to sit in on the interview, but their concerns about gotcha journalism vanished when they met Carolyn.

Tareq sat in a striped armchair in the living room. Carolyn set up the camera and gave Tareq a microphone. He ran the wire under his sweater and clipped it at the collar.

"So," Carolyn began, "tell me about life in Syria."

Carolyn expected to interview a frightened and tired man. Instead, she found someone only a few years younger than herself who was happy and eager to talk. He calmly told her about the destruction of the family home and the rocket attack that nearly killed him and his brother and precipitated the family's flight to Lebanon. He spoke for thirty minutes, answering each question thoughtfully and articulately. Robert, who had heard the story a dozen times already, listened rapt, like it was a radio drama.

"I've done my research, and I know you need doctors. I'm going to do it," Tareq told Carolyn. "I'm going to finish my medical degree."

He described the surprise welcome at the Halifax airport. "When I saw that view, it was the moment of my life. I can't express how this moment touched my heart," he said. "I walk out now, and because I'm the celebrity of the town everyone comes and asks me if I need any help," he laughed. "I am so grateful for the kind people here in Antigonish." Carolyn asked him what he would say to those still caught in the storm of war. "For refugees who are coming, I just want to say, there is always light in the dark. There is always hope in the frustration. Have faith. You will be safe here in Canada."

This man has a bright future, Carolyn thought. The interview over, she packed up and said goodbye. Before she got back on the road, she called her news editor.

"Nancy, you won't believe this guy. You won't believe the story he told. This guy's going to be our health minister in no time!"

Carolyn's interview with Tareq was so compelling that the broadcaster's flagship evening news program, the *National*, ran it, sharing the Hadhad story with viewers across the country. The CBC had found just the family it would follow for the year.

Seven

Shahnaz's heart now beat on two continents. She savoured the messages and conversations she had with Tareq. The photos he sent of Antigonish in the summer made her smile; she didn't let on that she'd already learned enough about Canada to know what it was really like in Nova Scotia in December. She yearned to see him again. If their visa ever came through, she, Isam, and their three youngest children would accept the opportunity to join Tareq in Canada. That would mean leaving their daughter Alaa and her two young children alone in Lebanon. It would mean moving farther from Walaa, who was living with her husband in Saudi Arabia, and Shahnaz's parents, siblings, and eldest daughter, all still in Damascus.

Batoul also missed Tareq. Seeing and hearing him by phone warmed her heart. Life in Saida was hard. Their apartment was small and lacked running water. A water truck drove along the street outside the apartment each morning, and Batoul's job was to run down to buy as many bottles as her family could afford. It was their only source of water for drinking, cooking, and cleaning. Even Lebanese citizens struggled with the country's widespread poverty and political instability. Jobs were scarce. Batoul knew many young Lebanese people who were eager to start a new life elsewhere.

Life in the refugee camps was even worse. The camps were a mess of muddy pathways and dirt roads packed with tarps and wood houses. Heavy old tires sat on roofs, put there to keep the metal from blowing away. Some people burned diapers to stay warm. A huge fire had ripped through one camp, destroying homes and killing an infant. A winter snowfall crushed roofs. Everyone wanted to be somewhere else: in Europe, in North America, or back in Syria. But Batoul was still apprehensive about moving across the world to live in a country that she could only imagine as unrelentingly cold; a place where everyone spoke a different language, followed a different religion, wore different clothes, and had different ideas. And yet the thought that Canada might never call, that they might not be reunited with Tareq, was equally painful.

Once Tareq left, everyone stayed close to home. Isam stopped going out to work. Tareq had received little notice before his flight, and they felt they had to be ready to go. They had heard of families who couldn't get to the airport in time to catch their flight and lost the opportunity. Isam clung to his Samsung phone like a life jacket. He kept it by his head when he slept and in his pocket during the day. Sometimes he took it out and put it on the table, just to keep a closer eye on it. He even took it into the bathroom when he washed up. He obsessively checked the charge level and signal strength, waiting, always waiting, for the call that would summon his family back to life.

In Syria, the killing continued. At the start of December, the United Kingdom sent fighter jets to bomb sections of the country thought to hold Islamic State fighters, adding to the three thousand French and American airstrikes that had already blitzed the land. Russia fought from the east, devastating towns suspected of disloyalty to al-Assad. Homs, Idleb, and Aleppo suffered the worst. Both German and Israeli soldiers moved in. People feared the civil war could blow up into a world war.

One Sunday in Ariha, a town in the north, three missiles exploded in a busy market, killing forty-nine civilians. Another day in December, the al-Assad regime bombed Douma, a suburb of Damascus not far from the Hadhads' old home. The attack killed forty civilians and injured seventy more. Then the government attacked southern Damascus, killing seventeen people and destroying homes and shops. Russian attacks in Aleppo killed eight, including four children.

Living as a refugee in Lebanon was like living in a flood. The water was right under your chin, and an extra wave of trouble could drown you. Shahnaz wanted to bring her family to higher ground. The destruction of the chocolate factory broke something in Isam, but it woke something in Shahnaz. In Syria, Isam had carried the family dream, building the home and the business that sustained them all, and now it was Shahnaz's turn. She trusted that Allah would help them to rebuild their lives. She was confident that, eventually, they would reach Canada. They would build a new chocolate company. "We will live in Canada," she assured her husband and children.

Coincidentally, just a few days before Tareq did his first interview with the CBC in Antigonish, a reporter for Radio-Canada, the CBC's French-language arm, interviewed his family in Saida. The reporter, working on a story about the Syrians stuck in limbo in Lebanon, waiting for word from Canada, picked the Hadhads at random. She interviewed them in their apartment, sitting on their red- and yellow-striped couch. They looked exhausted. Isam and Shahnaz said they hoped to reach Canada soon. Alaa explained she would be staying behind with her young children because she was in Lebanon on a tourist visa and was not recognized as a refugee. Shahnaz broke down in tears. Taghrid and Ahmad squirmed. Batoul stared at the floor.

It was early in January and Isam was standing in line, waiting to renew his six-month residency permit, when he received the phone call he feared might never come. An official at the Canadian embassy told him that he, his wife, and their three youngest children would leave for Canada on January 5. Isam did not bother to renew his permit. He raced home to tell his family.

❖

Tareq was standing in the Serses' kitchen, learning how to cook lentils by watching a YouTube video. He had rinsed the lentils and added water to the pot. Now he just had to figure out how to turn on the stove. A call from Lebanon interrupted his cooking lesson.

"*Marhaba*," Isam said. "We will be in Nova Scotia soon."

Tareq shouted with delight. He jotted down their travel dates and said goodbye. He messaged his friends from SAFE to share the good news with them, and then he turned his mind to all the things he needed to do. The first order of business was to make sure the yellow house was ready for their arrival, so Tareq got in touch with Heather Mayhew and Frank Gallant. On the day of the family's arrival, they picked Tareq up and drove him to their rental property on Bay Street. The driveway was still full of snow from the last storm, so Frank parked on the street. Across the street from the house was the hospital. Tareq saw that as an encouraging sign. He could imagine taking the short walk up the small hill to work.

They crunched across the yard through thick snow. Big evergreen trees huddled in front of the house, blocking much of the front window. They went inside the house, and Frank went to turn the heat on. Immediately inside the front door was a foyer with a staircase leading upstairs to the bedrooms and bathroom. To the right was a large furnished living room. An archway connected the living room to the dining room, which was dominated by a table big enough to accommodate their family. It reminded Tareq of the table they'd gathered around in their Damascus home. A large glass door led onto the deck. Tareq looked out at the expanse of snow. Beyond the deck, the backyard dropped off into a gully.

The dining room opened into the kitchen. A narrow door led from the kitchen to the basement. Frank and Heather told him it was unfinished but good for storing things. They creaked up the wooden stairs to the bedrooms on the second floor. Tareq quickly picked his own room and put down his bag.

It was so different from a Syrian home. Tareq ran his hand over the walls. He wondered how the thin wood kept the house warmer than thick concrete could. Syrian floors were usually tiled or covered with rugs, but the floors of the Antigonish house were bare wood. And, except for the occasional loud truck passing by, it was so quiet. Damascus never slept; you always heard the babble of life.

Back at the front door, Frank pointed to the snow-covered walk and driveway. "Guess who's going to shovel this?" he asked.

"I guess it's me!" Tareq laughed. When the driveway and front path were clear of snow and the house was warm and inviting, Frank, Heather, and Tareq locked the doors and said goodbye. Bronwen and her husband picked Tareq up in their minivan and started the drive to the Halifax airport. Tareq had not been able to assemble the crowd of six hundred that he'd promised his father, but a dozen friendly people from SAFE jumped at the chance to greet the Hadhads. It was only two weeks since Tareq had arrived in Halifax, but already it felt like a lifetime ago.

✦

The Hadhads' joy was mixed with sorrow. Joining Tareq in Canada meant saying goodbye to Alaa and her children, Sana and Omar. Alaa's husband was still missing, and she was still in Lebanon on a tourist visa. They worried that leaving would put her in danger. With her parents and siblings leaving, Alaa found a cousin willing to take her and her children in. It would be the first of many temporary homes.

The Hadhads packed their suitcases with a few changes of clothes and small sentimental items. Alaa took her pick of what remained but, with her future uncertain, she was reluctant to take much. Her parents gave away their remaining possessions and got their paperwork ready. Finally the day came when they had to say goodbye. Isam and Shahnaz hugged their daughter, kissed their grandchildren, and pledged that one day soon they would be together in Canada. Alaa held Sana and Omar tight and watched the taxi take her parents and siblings away.

Isam was taking no chances. He insisted they arrive at the airport on January 4, a full day before their departure, and sleep at the airport. The next day, tense with anticipation and lack of sleep, they boarded the flight for Jordan. They'd have a six-hour wait before getting on their flight to Toronto. On the plane, Shahnaz recalled the day nearly thirty years earlier when she'd missed what would have been her first flight. That had led her to the chocolate shop, to Isam, and to her future. Now here she was, experiencing flight for the first time in her life.

Isam watched out the window nearly the whole trip from Jordan to Toronto, seeing the beige land of the Middle East yield to the green world of Europe and then the vast expanse of the blue ocean. Snowy Labrador gave him his first glimpse of Canada. In Toronto, Isam parked himself at a window to watch planes take off and land. He'd never wanted to travel before, but now he found himself hypnotized by the easy way people left one world and landed in another. As he tracked a plane taxiing toward the gates, he felt something in himself settle. The long flight from danger was almost over. He was bringing his family to safety. He could build something new in this country. The ground would not shake. The buildings would not crumble. He asked Shahnaz if she wanted to count planes with him. She declined, but his happiness made her happy. Finally, it was time to board the flight to Halifax.

❖

It was a bitterly cold night in Halifax. Tareq and the SAFE volunteers chatted. He spotted Carolyn Ray, the CBC reporter, and went over to say hello. She had arranged to work this unusually late shift so she could capture the family reunion. Her instincts told her the Hadhad story was just beginning. Camera operator Steve Berry joined her, and the *National* planned to include the reunion in its next broadcast.

The group waited anxiously, checking the arrivals board until they saw the flight land. As passengers made their way from the gate to baggage claim, some glanced curiously at the TV crew and the welcome signs. The SAFE volunteers had learned a welcome chant in Arabic. Their pronunciation was imperfect, but their voices were warm and enthusiastic. After several long minutes had passed, Tareq spotted his younger brother. Ahmad paused and scanned the room. When he saw Tareq, he ran into his arms. Lucille Harper beamed and fought back tears as the brothers tightly embraced.

"Where are the others?" Tareq asked. Ahmad pointed behind him. Soon Batoul emerged. She smiled as she hugged Tareq, but the sea of smiling faces and the rapid-fire English that she couldn't understand overwhelmed the sixteen-year-old. Next came Isam, exhausted and unshaved, and then Taghrid. Tareq picked her up for a deep hug. Then, at last, it was his mother's turn. She hugged him, kissed him twice, closed her eyes, and inhaled his scent.

Carolyn Ray, mindful of her reportorial obligations, asked Tareq if she could interview his family.

"Batoul speaks English!" Tareq said. "You can talk to her."

Batoul looked terrified at the prospect. She was already feeling as though she'd been studying some other English for all those years. The only thing Shahnaz could remember how to say was thank you. She said it over and over again. Isam, worried about how he would sound in English, spoke through Tareq.

"I can now protect my family," he said. "We've done it. We've made it. I really want to get back to work." When Carolyn asked him what he did, Isam replied in English: "Chocolate." Switching back to Arabic, he explained: "We owned a chocolate-making business. We had a chocolate factory. We are now arranging here for starting a business. I find this is the country of opportunities."

As they headed out of the terminal, the newly arrived Hadhads gasped at the -14°C temperature. It had been 24°C when they left Lebanon. Isam fell deeply asleep on the drive to Antigonish. He could rest now that he'd gotten his family to safety and reunited with his eldest son.

It was four o'clock in the morning when the Hadhads reached the yellow house and Tareq could truly welcome them home.

Eight

When Shahnaz woke on her first day in Canada, her body creaked with the cold and her brain struggled with jetlag. She pushed off the heavy blankets and pulled open the curtains to look out her bedroom window. A winter wonderland greeted her. No apricot trees bent into her room. The evergreens danced in the wind and falling snow.

"How pure it is," she said to Isam, who was still buried under the covers. "It's coming from the sky. It's white and just touching the ground."

When they were both out of bed they dressed, checked on Taghrid and Ahmad, and headed downstairs. They'd arrived so late that they had barely seen the house before they went to bed. Isam fumbled with the locks on the front door and opened it, letting in a frosty wind. They stared in disbelief: two feet of snow blocked the way out. Shahnaz pulled on her winter coat and boots and started shovelling. Isam took the hint and joined her, but they struggled to clear even a narrow walking path.

"Isam, when will that end?" Shahnaz asked, pointing at the snow. He could only shrug.

Batoul had tossed and turned all night, sleeping occasionally and then waking up with a start. Questions raced through her mind. What were the schools like? What could she study? Would she make friends? Could they become citizens here? Would she have to move again? She pictured her sister Alaa, without her husband and now without her family, and wanted to be with her.

Batoul slid out of bed and walked to the window with a shiver. "Am I in Canada now?" she whispered to herself. The street was buried in snow. Her parents were haphazardly throwing snow off the driveway. She tried to open the window but couldn't lift it. A snowplow thundered by. *It's a hard thing*, she thought. *I will have to work hard in my new life in Canada to be a strong person.*

She dressed, went downstairs, and found Tareq. He told her other Arabic speakers and Muslim families lived in the area, and that brought her some comfort. "How do I speak English?" she asked him. "I want to speak English, to have conversations with Canadian people."

Tareq told her not to worry. "I will be your translator. You will learn English at school," he said with a smile. "You will make new Canadian friends. You will keep up the good things."

Frank and Heather stopped by later that day and found the Hadhads still valiantly trying to clear the driveway. Frank took charge, showing them how to push the snow over the bank instead of piling it at the sides, where it would only accumulate into high banks and make future clearing next to impossible. More snow was coming, Frank warned. He was right: that year, blizzards hit Nova Scotia on a nearly weekly basis, dumping mountains of snow in one of the heaviest winters the locals could remember.

On another January morning, Shahnaz arose early and, as was her custom, went to the window. Snow drifted down gently, covering the deck, decorating the evergreen trees, and filling the wooded gully at the end of the yard. Frank had told her she could turn the gully into a garden. She wondered how long it would take for all this snow to melt.

The sun had not yet risen, but its first rays illuminated the horizon and added a shade of blue to the snow. Then she spotted a darker shade in the shadows of the woods. Three shapes were slinking among the trees. She strained her eyes in the dawn and thought of waking Isam but decided to let him sleep. When she looked back out the window, it took a moment to find the trio. It was hard to guess their size in the unfamiliar landscape. Her research on Nova Scotia had told her the province was home to black bears. She knew they slept during winter, yet she also knew mother bears had their cubs in January and February.

She went down to the kitchen to make breakfast for her family. Tareq rose, rubbed a sleepy hand through a tangle of hair, and came into the kitchen. Batoul and the younger children stirred and came downstairs, shivering in the cold. In the basement, the furnace turned oil into heat and did its best to chase winter out of the house.

"I saw three bears," Shahnaz told them as they ate. She added, "I'm afraid of bears."

Everyone ran to look outside, scanning the trees for bears. Tareq researched them on his phone and set no one at ease with the information that black bears can weigh four hundred pounds and run fifty-six kilometres an hour. When Frank stopped by later that morning, Shahnaz told him what she'd seen. He seemed skeptical. He'd only seen a few bears in Antigonish in his entire life, so it seemed to him unlikely that the Hadhads would run into them mere weeks after landing.

"The bears should be hibernating," he explained. Shahnaz described the trio of hunched-over, furry creatures. Frank used his phone to search for pictures of a more likely candidate, showing Shahnaz a photo of a raccoon. Isam and Tareq were relieved. Shahnaz was not so sure, but she put it out of her mind. Animal predators worried her less than human ones.

Gradually, the Hadhads became more comfortable in their new home. They learned how to navigate a Canadian grocery store. They learned all the varieties of cold, from the dry cold that made their faces ache to the damp cold that chilled their bones so deeply that no thickness of sweater could keep them from shivering. They learned what a difference the wind could make: a temperature that was tolerable with just a coat and hat became unbearable in a howling blast of wind. They learned that snow came in different types, too. There was the crisp, white snow with a crust they could walk on top of until it broke and they dropped down a few inches, leaving rounded footprints. Sometimes the snow was damp and crumbly, like sand soaked by the rising tide, but it hid the treacherous ice beneath. Hard, brittle snow formed rigid dunes. Snowball snow was just damp enough to pack into balls. Flaky snow was too dry to stay together but perfect to catch on their tongues. They also learned how Canadians walked like penguins to avoid slipping on ice, keeping both feet in full contact with the ground at all times, sliding one foot and then the other, and keeping their centre of gravity low and balanced.

In the first two weeks, Batoul spent much of her time at Antigonish's public library, working on her English-language skills in preparation for the day when she would start school. When that day came, Batoul couldn't believe how long it took her and her mother to bundle Ahmad and Taghrid against the cold outside. First, they dressed in the clothes they'd picked out for the first day of school. Then came the serious dressing: heavy winter boots to grip icy sidewalks and kick through snowbanks; thick sweaters to hold body heat; heavy winter coats zipped all the way to the chin; scarves, hats, and mittens. They had to pack a pair of indoor shoes, too, so the snowy boots didn't make a mess of the classroom. She felt like an astronaut preparing for a spacewalk. In Syria they could wear the same clothes all day, indoor and out, and nobody had central heating.

Batoul had to tell herself daily that she would not freeze solid. She had feared the Canadian winter all the way from Lebanon, and it was as bad as she had dreaded. Canadian snow stacked up like bricks, forming walls everywhere. She stared in amazement as steam puffed out of her mouth when she spoke outdoors.

The big yellow bus arrived and stopped opposite the house. Batoul led her siblings across the street and onto the bus. Most of the students on the bus were younger than sixteen. Some looked surprised to see new faces. A few offered friendly smiles. Batoul and her siblings sat down in an empty row, and the bus rumbled back into motion.

Batoul should have been shaking with nerves. People at the library had kept asking her if she was nervous about starting school. She wasn't. She was excited.

The bus headed into town on a road lined with trees that winter had stripped bare. Snow buried their roots and clung to their branches. It seemed impossible that the trees were only sleeping, not dead. The bus driver stopped at the rail line and checked for trains before bumping over the tracks and into town. Batoul saw a store selling green tractors and then a restaurant she'd already heard a lot about: Tim Hortons. They crossed a short bridge over a pretty river banked with snow. Charming two-storey brick buildings lined Main Street. Batoul imagined the photos she could take of her new homeland. It was all much calmer and quieter than Damascus.

They reached Ahmad and Taghrid's school first. Batoul could tell they were nervous. This would be the first time they'd be away from the family. She said a few words of encouragement and was relieved to see smiling teachers greet them when they stepped off the bus. Batoul smiled and waved as the bus drove off. They looked so little as they walked with the teachers into the school.

The bus, now nearly empty, continued its journey to Dr. John Hugh Gillis Regional High School. They passed St. Francis Xavier University, a campus of snow-covered lawns, trees, and stately brick buildings trimmed in white. The bus turned off Main Street and entered a residential neighbourhood. The houses were cozy and small and on large pieces of land. Finally, the bus passed a large athletic field and pulled into the busy high school parking lot. Batoul picked up her things, tightened her clothes against the cold billowing in through the open door, and stepped outside. She was alone. When was the last time she had been alone? She couldn't remember. She liked the feeling. She could follow her own thoughts, which were an excited jumble of dreams for the future and grief for the past.

Hundreds of students walked into the high school, some glancing quickly at her. She didn't see another non-white student. Her first class didn't start for forty minutes, and no teachers were waiting to guide her inside and explain everything. She hesitated. A girl about her age approached. Dark curly hair snuck out from under her hat.

"I'm Carly," she said.

"I am Batoul," Batoul replied slowly.

Carly was Frank and Heather's daughter, but she'd not yet met the Hadhads. She told Batoul that she knew of one other student in the high school who spoke Arabic, a girl from Palestine, and promised to introduce Batoul to her. As Batoul removed her winter gear she noticed she alone, among the one thousand students, was wearing a hijab.

Carly gestured toward the cafeteria and invited Batoul to join her and her friends before class. Batoul slowly relaxed with Carly and her friends. She insisted she could follow the conversation. But when someone cracked a joke and everyone burst out laughing—everyone but Batoul—the isolation of language became clear. They would try to explain the joke, but no joke survives explanation.

Day by day, the Hadhad children settled into their new lives. Ahmad and Taghrid made friends. Batoul looked forward to chatting with Carly and her friends in the cafeteria each morning, and it wasn't long before Batoul started shepherding her sister and brother over toward Carly and sitting beside her on the bus. Her non-Muslim classmates marvelled at how she wore her hijab even while working up a sweat in gym class. Carly grew to respect the quiet conviction with which Batoul stuck to her values, even when other students stared at her curiously. She also stuck to several layers of clothing, no matter how warm it got. It was as if the Canadian winter had frozen her core and she could never quite thaw it.

One morning Batoul shyly pulled out her phone and showed Carly a photo of a nearby beach.

"You took this?" Carly asked. Batoul nodded.

Carly realized her new friend had an eye for photography. Despite her hatred of the cold, Batoul found herself drawn to the winter beach. Something about its austere majesty appealed to her, and she captured the way the sun played on the sand and water. Everything filled her with awe. She processed her new home photo by photo.

The high school students had studied the Syrian war and discussed what it meant to be a refugee. At Christmas, Carly's English class had purchased gifts to give to the Syrian students they knew would soon arrive. When that day finally came, the teachers realized what an enormous challenge it would be to teach math and science to students who spoke little or no English. Heather Mayhew was one of many volunteers who offered to help tutor the Syrian students after school. Many teachers, too, put in extra hours after school to help the students catch up.

Carly offered to tutor Batoul at the public library. She booked a room every Tuesday and Thursday after school where they could work. Carly was the only student to volunteer. She wished more of her classmates would join her. The adult tutors certainly knew the subjects, but they had forgotten what it was like to be a student. Carly admired Batoul's commitment, enthusiasm, willingness to work, and gratitude for the chance to learn. But she noticed that Batoul would nod and say, "Yes, yes, I understand," even if she didn't understand. It was as though she didn't want to say no to anything.

"It's okay to tell me you don't understand," Carly assured her.

Batoul hid her frustrations well. The English she had studied in Syria and Lebanon was slow and clear. Now she felt herself in the midst of a torrential river of words. And her English teachers back home had been Arabic speakers; she hadn't had the additional challenge of understanding a Canadian accent. It was an exhausting process: think a thought in Arabic, translate it into English, hear the response in English, and translate that into Arabic. The teachers were patient and spoke slowly, making sure she understood the material. They asked her questions and waited for her to answer and then ask questions of her own. Slowly, she untangled the new language.

Batoul talked to friends and family in Syria and Lebanon every day. They updated her on the latest war news: on who had fled, on who had died, and on how they persisted, nevertheless. She told them about her war with winter. Her friends back home gasped at her stories and admired her courage. Instead of brooding on what had been lost, she walked forward to take what the future offered.

She found the Canadian students friendly and curious. She used a translator on her phone to help her speak, and Carly introduced her to new people and told them a bit of her story. Her new friends learned to speak to her slowly, watching her eyes to see if she understood. She met the Palestinian girl, who had moved to Nova Scotia with her family a few years earlier. It was a relief to speak Arabic with her. She understood Batoul's situation, and they became close friends.

Within weeks of their arrival in Antigonish, every Hadhad seemed focused on the future. Batoul, Ahmad, and Taghrid had settled into school. Tareq was investigating what he needed to do to complete medical school so he could become a doctor. Shahnaz woke early to clean the kitchen, make breakfast, and prepare the younger kids for their school day. Then she cleaned, cooked, and messaged her daughters in Syria, Lebanon, and Saudi Arabia. The only exception was Isam. What would a middle-aged man with a jumble of skills and a passion for chocolate do when he had to start over in a strange country? Isam, who had always trusted his inner guide, suddenly felt as though he was lost in a dark wood, unsure of his next step.

He woke at strange times, in unexpected darkness or light, as his body kept the ancient rhythms of Damascus. He had been the family's breadwinner his entire adult life and he was hungry for work. But what could he do in this small town? It already had all the plumbers and electricians it needed. Besides, he couldn't make English words do what he wanted them to do. He spoke only to his family.

A few times a week, Isam walked into town. As he crossed the train tracks and passed the tractor store, he met people. He perked up, smiling, nodding, and exchanging greetings. He passed the Ford dealership and the tennis courts buried in crisp snow. A Canadian flag fluttered in front of the courthouse, a small, handsome wood building with four Ionic columns. Isam stepped carefully on the salted sidewalk. He went into the library. Local people, many of them retired, had volunteered to tutor the newcomers in English. Isam worked hard to express himself in the new language.

But as January turned into February, Shahnaz saw that her husband was still struggling. In the blank white snow of Canada, he saw no signs of his former self. When she had met him, he was a young chocolatier with a big dream. Now he was an older man with ruined dreams. She knew they must start a new chocolate company. Tareq was learning how hard it would be to retrain himself as a Canadian doctor. The country was full of taxi drivers who were engineers and lawyers in their home countries. But chocolate tastes sweet on all tongues. Shahnaz had seen the potential for chocolate from the moment Tareq first talked about emigrating to Canada.

"We can rebuild—and quicker than before, better than before," she told her husband. "Maybe you can meet Justin Trudeau." Isam laughed at the idea of meeting the prime minister over chocolate. "You never know where this will lead us," Shahnaz insisted. "This will be big."

Winter buried the land outside her window. She knew the hard snow would melt. The spring sun would turn it into nurturing water and the seeds would sprout.

Isam bought the ingredients he would need to make chocolate. When the children were out at school, he found a bowl in the kitchen and mixed the cocoa, sugar, and milk. He poured water into a large pot and brought it to a boil. He slid the bowl on top of the bubbling water and slowly stirred the paste until it was brown and smooth. He carefully removed the bowl from the stove and paused, looking for something that would serve as a mould. His eyes rested on an ice-cube tray. He set the bowl down, cleaned the tray, and placed it by the stove. He lifted the bowl again and poured out the rich mix of chocolate. He added pistachios and hazelnuts and covered them with warm chocolate. He carefully cleaned excess chocolate from the tray and slid it into the fridge. He sat down and waited for three hours, listening to Syrian music. He pulled the trays from the fridge and popped out the chocolates. He sampled one with a smile. When Frank stopped by, Isam offered him a chocolate.

Frank had been preparing for this encounter for a long time, though he never knew it. As he approached the middle years of his own life and his children grew up, he began to think about what truly counted. He devoted his professional life to helping companies, governments, and organizations figure out how to improve and achieve their goals. He specialized in helping people understand themselves and how they thought, so that they could be effective in all aspects of their lives. "We want to help you understand you better than anybody else in the world," he would say. Frank found James Hollis's book *The Middle Passage: From Misery to Meaning in Midlife* particularly helpful as he navigated this stage.

Since the Hadhads arrived in Nova Scotia, Frank had been trying to engage Isam, catching his eye, speaking in simple English. Frank even learned a few Arabic phrases. Isam used his broken English, his translator son, and his phone to share his difficulties. Frank saw something in Isam's struggle that he recognized in himself. He decided to spend more time with Isam, despite the awkward language barrier.

Frank noticed the dirty bowl and tray and the chocolate splattered around the kitchen. Everyone in his family loved chocolate, and he often bought ten-kilogram bags of the best chocolate he could find. It was a leftover habit from the days when he was first courting Heather. Carly was in grade nine when she decided to use the chocolate to make truffles. She planned to eat the entire batch herself, and her brothers dubbed her the Truffle Troll for hoarding the sweets. Carly relented—the truffles were really too rich for just one person. Her family loved them, but Carly, wanting an unbiased opinion, got her older brother, Morgan, to take some to work with him. His colleagues not only devoured the truffles but gave him money to pay Carly. Morgan urged her to think about making more and selling them at the farmers' market.

Encouraged, Carly bought more ingredients from the grocery store. It took her around two hours to make two hundred truffles. She packed them in clear plastic containers, priced them at six for five dollars, and rented a stall at the Antigonish Farmers' Market. She unfurled a Truffle Troll banner on the front of the table. She sold out in two hours. Soon Carly was not only selling chocolate at the market each week but also providing truffles to weddings and other special events. She listened to her customers and expanded her product line, offering dark chocolate, mint, cookie dough, peanut butter, cappuccino, Oreo cheesecake, and maple truffles. At times of peak demand, like Christmas, she could spend thirty or forty hours a week making a thousand truffles. She received the Antigonish Chamber of Commerce's first Young Entrepreneur Award in recognition of her booming business.

Frank could see by the Hadhads' messy kitchen that Isam truly loved making chocolate, and it occurred to him that if Carly could operate a successful truffle business, Isam could probably get Hadhad Chocolate off the ground again, at least in a small way. He and Carly decided to give Isam several kilograms of raw chocolate to get him started. He beamed when he received the gift. He asked for dried lemons and oranges and some crunchy nuts, and while they went shopping, he pulled out the big pot and bowl and heated water on the stove. He placed the raw chocolate in the bowl and slid it on top of the pot.

The hot water slowly melted the chocolate. When Frank and Carly returned with the dried fruit and nuts, he poured the mix into the ice-cube trays, added the nuts, topped them off with more chocolate, and set them in the fridge to cool and harden.

The familiar happiness returned: the pleasure of work, the joy of the smells, and the delight of people anticipating the finished chocolates. He could say everything he needed to say in chocolate. The magic of chocolate was just as powerful here as it had been decades earlier, when he stood in his mother's messy kitchen and watched her bite into his first chocolates.

Frank and Carly sampled the chocolate with approval. Isam had started with nothing more than a dream of spending his life making chocolate, and he'd built that into a thriving international business that supported his family and provided employment for many others. He began to believe he could do it again.

Isam spent many happy hours making chocolate in the kitchen of his snow-covered Antigonish home, the windows steamed up, Syrian music playing on his phone. Years of anger and frustration receded into the past. He produced hundreds of delicious Syrian chocolates. They were darker and harder than a typical Canadian chocolate. The nuts and dried fruit gave them a unique taste. Isam knew the secret ingredient was always happiness.

Word spread through Antigonish that the new Syrian family was making chocolate. Perfect strangers started knocking on their door. Tareq or Isam would answer with a smile. The strangers would grin awkwardly, mention chocolate, and offer them cash. It made Isam so happy that he didn't want to taint it with money, so he started handing out treats like it was Halloween.

A polite stampede started. A few people, knowing only that they were looking for a yellow house on Bay Street, knocked on the door of a bright yellow one half a block down. Fortunately, the people who lived there were happy to take on the civic duty of redirecting callers to the Hadhad home. Only around 10 per cent of Antigonish's population had played some role in getting the Hadhads to Nova Scotia. Now, everyone wanted to help them succeed, especially if it meant buying chocolate, but Isam continued to refuse payment. It made him happy to have something to give.

Somehow, a chocolate maker in Montreal got word of Isam's story and tracked down the Hadhads. He spoke to Tareq on the phone.

"Would your father like to move to Montreal?" the man asked.

"We can help build a factory and go into business with him." Tareq said he would talk to his family and call the man back.

Tareq knew what his family would say before he asked them, but he asked anyway. Although they'd only been in Antigonish a few weeks and could see the advantages a cosmopolitan city could offer them, the Hadhads recognized that people in Montreal hadn't helped bring them from Lebanon to Canada. Montrealers weren't donating time, money, and resources to help them build new lives.

"No, we are not leaving Antigonish," Tareq told the man. "The town really invested in us with kindness and welcome. We are grateful to them. We will build our business in this town."

Isam started leaving the house more. He still struggled to learn English at the library, and after another Syrian family arrived, he found comfort in sitting with the other men, speaking Arabic outside of the classes. He felt more connected to his new home.

❖

Through the dark, wintry woods of Antigonish, people walked in pairs and small groups. They came from the campus of St. Francis Xavier University, from the side streets and the suburbs, drawn to the tall white steeple of St. James United Church on Main Street. The sunlight faded from the late February sky.

Inside the church hall, Jyotsna Jain checked again to make sure everything was perfect for the potluck. She watched her friends arrange chairs around tables and write names on nametags. Just a few weeks earlier, Nova Scotia's beloved groundhog Shubenacadie Sam had crawled out of his hole, looked around, and failed to see his shadow. That meant spring would come early.

Jyotsna hoped so. She and her husband had left their home in Bangkok in 2012 and immigrated to Antigonish. Before that, they had lived in Africa, the United States, and her native India. She had never seen snow before they moved to Nova Scotia. It charmed her—for the first three days. But she soon realized that hiding away only made the winter blues worse. She watched locals boisterously "take the roof off winter" by playing hockey on ponds, gathering for Christmas parades, and snowshoeing through the woods. She decided to follow their example.

She ran her idea past a group of friends she'd made, a mixture of locals and newcomers, and together they founded the International Potluck Group. They gathered each month from fall to spring. The potlucks were an instant hit, drawing all kinds of people for a mix of music, food, and dancing. One hundred people regularly came to the church hall. Statistics Canada would tell you that Antigonish was 90 per cent white and Catholic, but the potlucks revealed a different story. The university drew people from all over the world: Africa, India, the Middle East, Europe, Russia, South America, and China.

On this particular night, the International Potluck Group was looking forward to welcoming Antigonish's first Syrian families. As people filed into the hall, carrying Crock-Pots, casserole dishes, and sweets, Jyotsna kept watch for Tareq. He had agreed to speak to the group before they ate. People took the food to the kitchen, hung their winter coats over the backs of their chairs to claim them, stuck on their name tags, and started chatting with each other. Karen Foley, who had moved to Antigonish from Virginia only a few years earlier, was the first to spot the Hadhads. They arrived bearing chocolate.

Tareq stood comfortably at the front of the hall and talked about his family's journey to Canada. His grin came easily. He would later say it was around that evening that he began to feel as though he'd been born in Nova Scotia, whisked away to Syria as a baby, and that he had now returned home. He thanked the community for rescuing his family and for embracing them like sisters and brothers.

His poise impressed Karen. He was so wise and worldly for

such a young man. As soon as he finished speaking, she snatched a chocolate off the plate on the dessert table and popped it into her mouth. It was sweet and rich, filled with honey. The pile soon vanished.

Fran Wittgens watched her community embrace the Syrian newcomers, just as they had embraced her and her family when they arrived from the United States. She knew Antigonish had a history of welcoming immigrants, and she noticed that those in the previous generation of newcomers were always the most enthusiastic helpers of the next.

People asked Isam when he would make more chocolate and when he would start selling it. He shook his head at the idea of accepting money from the village that was doing so much for his family. He would, he insisted, keep giving the chocolates away.

Nine

Two women changed Isam's mind about selling the chocolates. When Carly heard about how everyone at the potluck had loved Isam's chocolates, she encouraged him to sell them at the indoor winter market. Shahnaz was also convinced that it was time to start selling. She and Isam wanted to be financially independent, and they wanted to be able to give back to the community, just as they had in Damascus. Earning money from the chocolates was the key. Carly gave Isam some of the paper cups she used in her truffle business and some clear plastic sandwich containers that could serve as the first chocolate boxes. Isam filled a box to see how it looked.

"Five dollars," he announced.

Frank shook his head. At that price, Isam would lose money on every box.

"These are good," Frank told him. "Sell them for ten or fifteen dollars."

Isam realized he needed to upgrade his equipment to keep pace. The ice-cube trays weren't cutting it. He asked Frank about getting a proper chocolate mould. Frank tried to find one in Halifax, but nobody had one. Online research revealed a company in Quebec that sold chocolate-making equipment, and Frank ordered five moulds. When he put the moulds on the Hadhads' kitchen table, Isam reached solemnly into his shirt pocket and pulled out a plain notebook. He carefully recorded what Frank had bought him and his debt of a few hundred dollars, and he left a blank spot where he would record repayment.

The Hadhad kitchen became an impromptu factory. Over the next week, every Hadhad worked to help Isam melt chocolate on the stove, mix in the right ingredients, and pour it into the new moulds to cool in the refrigerator. When it was ready, the younger children knocked the chocolates out of the moulds and into big plastic boxes. When Isam finally said they could stop, Batoul counted 150 boxes. They were ready for their first day at the market.

The winter market had opened the year before and its mix of vendors selling honey, fish, soaps, and crafts drew a good crowd. By the time the Hadhads opened their booth at 10 a.m., a long line had already formed. Frank was on hand to help the Hadhads and Carly, who set out her truffles. Isam's plan was to let customers choose each chocolate, assembling each box individually. That would slow sales, Frank pointed out.

"Sell them in pre-made containers," he advised.

Isam shook his head. "No, loose," he said.

Isam smiled at their first customer, gestured to the chocolates, and invited her to select hers. She did, and for the next two hours, Isam slowly welcomed each customer, hand-packed their chocolates, and parted with them warmly. They sold out before noon, leaving a long line of unfed people who made them promise to come back next week. Carly sold all of her truffles as well.

From early morning to late at night, Isam made chocolate. Frank delivered the raw ingredients early in the week, and Isam recorded the debt in his notebook. Chocolates filled the fridge. On weekends, Frank drove Carly, Isam, Tareq, and the chocolate to the market. Soon he had to make two trips: one to carry the people, and one to deliver the chocolate. Isam used his profits to repay Frank and purchase new ingredients. Tareq, who had never worked in his father's business in Syria, became his full-time interpreter.

The next pieces of equipment that Isam needed were a small fridge he could use just for cooling and storing chocolate, and a tempering machine. Mixing and melting chocolate by hand in a double boiler was imprecise. If Isam cooked it for too long, the chocolate would take on a dull and uneven colour streaked with grey. Worse, it would taste chalky and grainy. The tempering machine would heat the chocolate to an exact temperature, then cool and reheat it, all the while mixing it evenly. The finished chocolates would always be smooth and glossy. Frank found a supplier in Montreal and told them the Hadhads' story. The supplier offered a 20 per cent discount on the professional-grade tempering machine they needed, but it would still cost $3,500. Frank blanched. Then he talked to Heather.

"Do we want to loan Isam $3,500?" he asked her. It was a substantial sum, well beyond what he'd feel comfortable writing off if things didn't work out, and he worried about mixing business and friendship. Heather thought it was a worthwhile investment, however, so Frank ordered the machine. He had to drive to Truro to pick it up. When he delivered it to the Hadhad home, Isam invited Frank to join him in business.

"Partners? Partners, no friction," he said to Frank.

"No, the business is yours," Frank said. "We will just help."

Isam entered the debt into his book. Every week Frank delivered supplies, the Hadhads produced another batch of chocolate, and on weekends they sold it all at the market. Every week, Isam made another payment on his debt to Frank.

One weekend Tareq looked over at the different varieties of truffles that Carly was selling.

"What is this?" he asked her, eyeing a creamy truffle.

"Peanut butter and chocolate," she told him.

It sounded bizarre. Was she kidding him? She offered him one to try, and he took a cautious bite.

"No," he said immediately, putting the rest of the truffle down. There were some things about Canada he would never understand.

❖

Like Isam's mother before her, Shahnaz soon tired of having a chocolatier in her kitchen. She'd come downstairs on the mornings after market days to find dirty dishes filling the sink and covering the stove. Smears and drops of chocolate splattered on everything: the stove, the walls, the counters, the cupboard doors, the fridge. She still had to cook for the whole family. It was getting out of hand. She told Isam she was kicking him out of her kitchen.

Their success at the market and the steady stream of would-be customers at the front door convinced Isam that he could start a company in Antigonish, and with his wife's ultimatum in mind and Tareq translating, he asked Frank about moving the chocolate-making to a different location. Frank suggested they look in the basement. They went down the narrow steps. Tareq had to bend his neck to avoid hitting his head. Frank turned on the light to reveal an unfinished basement with a gravel floor and exposed vents and joists running across the ceiling.

A small room lit by a lone, exposed bulb was on the far side. It had been built to keep vegetables but now housed a broken vacuum cleaner and dead fan. The room was ten feet by six feet, and the ceiling was just a little taller than Tareq. The walls, the foundation of the house, were made of concrete. To Isam, it felt like he was standing in a corner of his Damascus factory. It was the perfect place to start over.

Isam and Tareq carried the heavy tempering machine down the stairs and into the new subterranean factory. Isam bought two card tables and a little fridge that could hold ten moulds at a time. Everything went into the cold-storage room. Isam covered the exposed insulation on the ceiling and blocked the one little window to keep the rare bursts of sun from affecting the chocolate. They attached shelves to the walls and installed a hot plate. Tareq found a green marker and wrote on the wall the word *Chocolate*.

"It is a reminder that this is a factory now," he told his family. "Don't put anything else here."

That night, Isam tempered and melted the chocolate before pouring it into moulds. Ahmad and Batoul filled them with nuts. Tareq put the moulds into the fridge. When they had set, Batoul knocked them out of the moulds. Everyone pitched in to help with "cupping," the slow job of putting one thousand individual chocolates into one thousand individual paper cups. The work left their hands aching and their necks stiff, but it made their hearts happy.

Isam could feel the engine of the business kicking into gear.

Frank started bringing sixty kilograms of cashews and pistachios at a time. If they could make two hundred boxes and sell them for ten dollars each, they could take in $2,000 at the market. Isam would carefully count out the money he owed Frank, pay him, record it in the book, and then invest the profits into growing the business. Frank and Isam had started to call it their friendship book, as each transaction reflected a deepening of their relationship. In late February, less than two months after their arrival in Antigonish, the Hadhads registered the business as Hadhad Chocolate.

Tareq received a phone call from Carolyn Ray, the CBC reporter. Carolyn had kept in touch, waiting for the right time to return and catch up with the Hadhads. In the weeks since they'd arrived, SAFE had welcomed two more families and was getting ready to bring another. Carolyn was sure this was the perfect time to do a story about the ongoing fundraising and the struggles of adjusting to life in a new country; a story with a tight focus on the Hadhads and their emerging chocolate business.

Carolyn and Steve Berry, the camera operator, arrived in March. They visited Lucille Harper at the Antigonish Women's Resource Centre. Lucille laughed when Carolyn reminded her that when they first spoke, SAFE's plan was to raise funds for three years and welcome one family. That was less than a year earlier, and already three families called Antigonish home and a fourth was on the way. Lucille said the newcomers had made the ongoing humanitarian disaster in Syria real for locals. What they saw on TV and online was no longer happening to distant strangers but to the friends and family of people they'd welcomed at the airport, eaten dinner with, and spoken to at community gatherings.

As she walked down Main Street, Carolyn observed how much joy people took in having the Syrians in town. Everyone she stopped to ask about the newcomers smiled and spoke with pride. No one seemed to resent them or to understand why any community would reject Muslim refugees. The new families were working and contributing to Antigonish, and outgoing Tareq in particular seemed to have met all four thousand permanent residents.

At St. Ninian's Church, Carolyn met a second group: Canadians Accepting Refugees Everywhere, or CARE. "Being a refugee is being a victim of circumstances. It's not a characteristic of who you are," CARE member Donna MacGillvray said. CARE had collected clothing and houseware donations and turned the basement of the church into a trendy boutique. Newcomers could choose whatever they wanted at no charge. Students at St. Francis Xavier University gave up one cup of coffee a day and in doing so raised thousands of dollars. Professors gathered money from unions and businesses. The town had raised more than $170,000 in under a year.

"We're not saving the six million Syrian refugees. We're not saving one million even, like the Germans are doing," said Michael Steinitz, a physics professor. "But in Antigonish, we're saving some."

Carolyn hoped to film Isam making chocolate, but when she and Steve stepped into the Hadhads' home, they found he had already finished for the day. Fruit, cookies, biscuits, and chocolate were spread on the dining-room table.

The camera delighted Ahmad and Taghrid, who eagerly showed off their games and toys. "We've never had board games before," Taghrid said. They challenged each other to see who could count the highest in English.

"The schools are different than in Syria," Ahmad said, his eyes shining, "because everything is amazing here. Amazing and fantastic."

Taghrid showed off her stuffed animals: a duck, a giraffe, and two monkeys. The nine-year-old introduced Carolyn to each animal. "This is Chocolate," she said, holding up one of the monkeys. The smile on her face matched the smiling emojis on the clips that pinned back her long hair.

"The gifts are amazing!" Taghrid said with bright eyes. Ahmad repeated her, carefully shaping each syllable: "Ah-maz-ing!"

Batoul was quieter than her brother and sister, but she shared that she was playing the flute at high school. She loved learning, she said, and finding the universal language of music filled her with joy.

"I am very happy for this house," Shahnaz said before dissolving in tears. She and Isam had expected to start life in Canada at zero, crammed into a tiny apartment in a crowded city. Instead, they were in a comfortable home in a friendly village that looked like something they'd seen in a Christmas movie on television. "Excuse me," she apologized, wiping the tears away. She gathered herself and showed Carolyn a prized possession: a photograph of a bird with a long, slender beak and an eye-catching mohawk of feathers. In English, the bird is known as the hoopoe. In Arabic, it is called the hadhad.

"It was like three years of depression and frustration, because I stayed at the house most of the time," Isam said of his time in Lebanon, speaking through Tareq. "The first months here have erased years of suffering. You know, in five or ten years, we will have a business." He opened the fridge to show the stacks of chocolates ready for the next market day.

But when Carolyn asked Tareq about his plans to become a doctor, frustration surfaced. When he'd had to leave Syria, he'd been a year away from completing medical school. He knew that Canada needed doctors, especially in rural communities, and he wanted to be one of those doctors. He'd hoped he could finish his last year of studies in Canada and start working. When he realized that his new home was directly across the street from a hospital, it seemed like destiny.

But he'd learned that Canada would not recognize any of his education or the volunteer work he'd done with the mobile clinic in Lebanon. He'd have to enrol as an undergraduate and spend three or four years earning a bachelor's degree before putting in several more years at medical school. The competition for places at Canadian medical schools was fierce, and students regularly spent a decade studying and graduated owing more than $150,000. Dalhousie University in Halifax, which had a medical school, said it was trying to accommodate refugee students like Tareq, but it could be close to a decade before he could begin practising medicine.

"I know that studying medicine here is so competitive for Canadians," Tareq told Carolyn. "But there really is a big lack of doctors here, so I really hope I can be helpful for the Canadians and for the Syrian refugees who arrived here lately. I didn't give up. I'm determined to continue medicine."

Still, a joke he'd learned from a Syrian friend living in Toronto resonated with him. The friend told him that if you were going to have a heart attack in Toronto, it was safer to do it in a taxi than an overcrowded emergency room, because so many of Toronto's taxi drivers were immigrant doctors.

In the meantime, he needed to think about the present. Looking for a job was, he thought, like following another car to find a parking spot in a busy lot: you'll never find an empty spot before the car ahead of you fills it. But if you followed your own instincts, it seemed to him, you had a better chance of finding a space. Tareq started to turn his mind toward entrepreneurship. He and his father liked a line from the American businessperson, Reid Hoffman, who defined an entrepreneur as someone who jumps off a cliff and builds a plane on the way down. To Tareq's way of thinking, he and his family had already jumped off the cliff—or been pushed off—and they might as well build their own plane.

Later, when Carolyn was back in the newsroom in Halifax, editing the story, she pulled up footage from the interview that Radio-Canada had done with the Hadhads, when they were still in Lebanon but hoping to join Tareq soon. Isam's appearance in the earlier interview shocked her. He looked pale and sick, like a late-winter tree. Since his arrival in Canada just two months earlier, he'd put on twenty pounds. He had colour in his face and a spark in his eye. He was budding with life.

❖

Shahnaz was grateful for her Antigonish home and happy to see Isam, in particular, renewing his purpose in life, but still her heart beat on two continents. She and Isam had left three adult daughters in the Middle East. Kenana, their eldest, was in Damascus with her husband and children. So far, they were safe. Walaa was in Saudi Arabia with her husband and was starting a family. They talked about one day emigrating to Canada, but they were not in any danger. It was Alaa, still unable to find out what had happened to her husband and taking care of her two young children, who preyed on Shahnaz's mind. Her first thought on waking was to calculate the time in Lebanon and wonder what they were doing. She texted her daughters every day and spoke to them almost as often, via WhatsApp phone calls or video chats.

Tareq was confident that Alaa, Omar, and Sana would join the Hadhads in Antigonish. He was working on their papers, trying to get them to Canada. Given the urgency, he was relieved when CARE said it could help right away, raised the needed $30,000, and agreed to take legal responsibility for bringing Alaa and her children to Canada.

In the meantime, Alaa lived precariously in Saida. She had put on a brave face when her parents and younger siblings left. She knew they must go, and she believed Tareq when he said they would bring her family to Canada one day. But the tourist visa she had arrived on had expired, and she and the children had no legal right to stay in Lebanon. Alaa thought of her husband constantly. It was a year since Mamdouh and his brothers had disappeared. Was he dead? Alive but lost in some government prison basement? Had he suffered? Would he one day get free and try to find her? Omar wept for his missing father nearly every day. Sana said little, which was equally troubling.

Every decision carried heavy consequences. Should she stay in Lebanon and risk an arrest that would leave her children entirely on their own? Pay a smuggler to get them to Europe and risk dying in the attempt? Return to Syria? These questions were too big for Alaa to answer. She focused on little questions instead, doing the next thing her children needed, providing them with food and drink when they were hungry and thirsty, and comfort when they cried in the night.

Unable to risk renting an apartment and exposing herself to the government, every few weeks she packed up her children's things and walked to the next temporary home.

And yet somehow she continued her studies at the college she'd attended with Batoul, and her children continued their elementary school education when they could. She told herself: Live your life with patience; we are going; we will follow them to Canada someday; the future will be bright for me and my children.

Whenever she could connect to Wi-Fi, she went on Facebook. She watched, amazed, as her family posted articles and news about the chocolate business. It delighted her to see her father expressing himself as a chocolatier again and succeeding in a country he knew nothing about, in a culture foreign to him, and in a language he barely understood. She imagined Omar taking over from his grandfather one day. She studied YouTube videos of people speaking English. She waited.

Ten

Neil Stephen's family moved to Antigonish when he was in tenth grade. He fell in love with the town. It helped that he met Kirsten at the same time and fell in love with her, too. They finished high school, attended university, graduated, married, and Neil founded his own marketing company in Halifax. They often returned to Antigonish to visit family.

The couple was driving along Main Street near the university and listening to the news on the radio. The last item was about the Syrian refugee family in Antigonish that was rebuilding their chocolate company. It immediately occurred to Neil that this was something he could help with: he could apply his marketing skills to help the Hadhads develop their brand. Kirsten thought it was a good idea. The pro bono work would be a gift to their hometown.

Unable to find a way to contact the Hadhads online, Neil sent a message to one of his first clients, Sean Fraser. Neil's company had worked with Fraser on his campaign to win the member of Parliament's seat for the area in the federal election the previous October. Neil was confident that Fraser would have come into contact with Hadhads, and he asked the MP to let them know that Neil wanted to help them. Tareq contacted Neil in April and asked him to help them come up with a company name that would capture their story.

Usually, Neil would spend months preparing before sitting down with a client, but this meeting had come about so quickly that he turned his thoughts to chocolate only as he pulled into the Hadhad driveway.

Neil and Tareq sat down at the dining-room table, and Neil asked about the chocolate factory. Tareq told him he was sitting on it. Tareq told Neil about the workforce (the family) and the business plan (sell chocolate at Antigonish's winter and summer markets). Neil thought that with hard work and some help from his team, the Hadhads could perhaps one day open an actual shop, and the business could grow to provide full-time jobs for Isam and Shahnaz.

Talk turned to the company name. "We totally want to connect the story to peace," Tareq said. "Because we lost everything in the war, and we could lose everything again here. You just don't know."

"Okay," said Neil. "So with that in mind, what would you call the company?"

Tareq paused and thought for a few moments. "The Hadhads Chocolate for Peace," he said. "Or Syrian Chocolate for Peace."

Neil shook his head. Those names were a bigger mouthful than a box of chocolates. It could take months to name a company, he said, and even then there was no guarantee that the name would do much for the business. But then Neil watched his own hands grab a piece of paper and scribble a three-word phrase. It hadn't been in his brain the second before, but there it was on the page. This flash of inspiration had never happened to him before, and he was fairly sure it would never happen again. But he knew he'd written the truth. He slid it across the table.

"Peace by Chocolate," Tareq read. "Oh. Okay, great, but it's a long name."

"You'll love it," Neil promised.

Tareq looked at the name again. He smiled. It was perfect.

May melted the last of the winter's great snowfall and started to coax green shoots out of the land. When Shahnaz pulled back her bedroom curtains in the morning, she took in leaves budding on trees, crocuses poking out of the ground, and the promising scent of spring. Batoul led her brother and sister to school in the morning in lighter gear.

Gradually, the Hadhads acquired more accoutrements of Canadian life. They purchased a 2006 Chrysler for $900, paying cash, and Tareq and Isam got Canadian drivers' licenses; Batoul got braces to straighten her teeth. Isam spent his days in the basement, happily making chocolates. Tareq ran the stall at the market.

Peace by Chocolate outgrew the basement. They spoke to Heather and Frank about expanding again. They raised the possibility of finishing the basement and turning it into a bigger factory, but Isam thought about Hadhad Chocolate's roots in a small factory and storefront back in 1986; how he'd met Shahnaz and started the family that now gave purpose to his life. His company in Syria had grown to the point where he rarely made the chocolate himself and no longer dealt directly with his customers. He wanted to return to the work of his younger self: making chocolate and meeting customers. Frank and Heather suggested they put a small shed on the property, next to the house.

Isam loved the idea. Tareq ordered dump-truck loads of gravel to build a base. The truck backed into the driveway and poured out the rocks. Ahmad became the chief leveller, leading Frank and Isam as they smoothed out the gravel into a compact pad. Tareq researched shed prices. Curious people in Antigonish saw the work, asked what they were up to, and volunteered to help. Some local families offered to fund an interest-free loan to help them buy the materials. The little group of angel investors stayed together to help other Syrians restart their lives in Antigonish County.

Tareq found a shed that seemed to be the right size at a price they could afford. While they waited for the seller to deliver it, a terrible wildfire started burning outside Fort McMurray, Alberta. It reached the community on May 3. Flames ripped through the booming oil town. Some eighty-eight thousand people fled, clogging the smoky roads. Firefighters, the Canadian Forces, and the RCMP tried to stop the blaze, but more than two thousand buildings were destroyed.

The Hadhads watched on TV as the Canadian families fled the danger and felt compelled to help. They met around the table and decided to donate May's profits to the Canadian Red Cross, which would use the money to help resettle the displaced people of Fort McMurray. Soon afterward, Carolyn Ray turned up at the market to record a radio story. As she was leaving, Tareq mentioned that they were donating their profits to Fort Mac. Carolyn was sitting in her car at a gas station when she realized what he'd told her. This family of refugees that had been in Canada for only five months was already reaching out to help others? She quickly typed up a story and emailed it to the web desk. She wasn't sure it would be posted to the site. Then she set off for Halifax. She was still on the highway when her phone started buzzing with so many incoming emails that she pulled over and snuck a look at it, fearing some catastrophe had struck. She saw her inbox was flooded with requests to buy chocolate.

By the time she reached Halifax, hundreds of thousands of people had read her story, and many of them wanted to support the Syrian chocolate family. But the Hadhads had no website, not even a Facebook page. Googling them produced Carolyn's stories and contact information. People from all over North America were emailing her to ask how to buy chocolates to help the family who was helping the Fort Mac families. Later that day, she checked her Twitter and noticed a member of the Prime Minister's Office was following her.

The donations story remained CBC Nova Scotia's most-read story for three full days. The only other story in her entire career that attracted more page views was an obituary for the beloved Cape Breton singer Rita MacNeil. A few weeks later, Al Jazeera interviewed Tareq about the donation.

"We really know the meaning of losing everything in one moment," he told their reporter. "To lose everything in one moment, you will lose your whole past, everything you have been building since you were born."

For the first time, the story of Peace by Chocolate found a global audience. Tareq started to realize that they were building something big.

❖

They waited all May, but the shed didn't arrive. Finally, on June 4, a truck pulled up with a pile of material in the back.

"It's not coming off the truck until you pay the full amount," the seller told them.

Frank helped them negotiate the seller down to a partial price, particularly since a closer inspection of the load showed that he hadn't brought the shed's door, windows, or roof. The seller dumped the goods in the yard and left, promising to bring the rest soon. He did not. The future home of Peace by Chocolate remained a small pile of building supplies stacked next to a gravel pad.

Frank stared at the pile of boards and tried not to feel overwhelmed.

"How do we take an empty shell and design it into a chocolate factory?" he asked.

Nobody had an answer ready, but they sat around the dining-room table and tried to figure it out. They needed enough space for Isam to work, as well as room for the tempering machine, fridge, and finished chocolates. Isam insisted on having a window at the front of the building where he could serve walk-up customers. They sketched out plans and Frank got on his phone to organize help. He spread the word through SAFE: the Hadhads were building a tiny factory.

That weekend, a volunteer crew of professional carpenters, electricians, and plumbers, plus a few general workers, started to raise the shed. One of them was Peter Wade, a retired engineer who enjoyed giving back to his community. When the Syrians started coming to Antigonish, he spent his days and evenings helping them settle. He was devoting most of his days to preparing a home for the next family due to arrive. A doctor owned the building and for years he had donated the space as a recovery centre for people recovering from drug addictions. The centre had moved on, so he'd recruited friends to turn it into a comfortable family home.

Peter would put in a full day's labour at that project, eat a quick meal, and drive over to help with the Hadhads' shed. Most of his professional engineering work had been far removed from actually building things. Working with his hands took him back to his childhood in Ontario, where his father and mother, scrappy English immigrants who came to Canada after World War II, taught him to waste nothing. They'd showed him what newcomers could do, and he wanted to help the Syrians do the same thing. He worked with Marty Alpert, an electrician who had upgraded other houses for the town's newcomers. Marty had been born in Brooklyn, New York, and took a "back to the land" trip to Nova Scotia in the 1970s. He stayed, adding to the roughly dozen Jewish people in Antigonish. "This project is proof that Jews and Muslims can get along," Marty said to

Peter with a grin. Peter thought the volunteers showed that people were willing to do a lot for chocolate—and even more for peace.

Isam offered the volunteers tea and chocolates. Ahmad smoothed the pile of gravel. He seemed to want to build a solid foundation for his family, just as his great-grandfather had done in Damascus years ago. Peter thought about what Isam said so often: he didn't make chocolate, but happiness. Peter realized helping the Syrians made him happier than he'd been in years. He particularly liked Tareq and was helping him to improve his English. Because Tareq was articulate and confident and smiled so much, people thought he understood what they were saying. In fact, he had confessed to Peter, he understood only about half of what was said to him. All the volunteers left happier than when they arrived. Peter thought, it was more than happiness: it was peace.

The shed became a factory. The doors and windows arrived. Only the roof remained missing. As the summer crept on, Frank and Tareq realized that they would have to go get the roof. They drove over to the shed shop in Frank's Prius, feeling slightly nervous, as though they were planning a burglary. They called the owner, texted him, and knocked on his office door, but he did not reply. They could see the roof. They had already paid for it. But if they took it, were they stealing? Frank tried calling the owner again, and this time he answered.

"I've found the roof. Can I take it?" Frank asked. The owner agreed, reluctantly, and they acted quickly before he could change his mind. They shoved the roof into the Prius. It barely fit, and then they realized they had to get themselves in, too. Frank slid in first, pushing the roof to the passenger's side to create room for him to sit in the driver's seat. Tareq laughed and did the limbo to get under the roof and into his seat.

"I finally have a roof over my head!" he joked.

Isam's smile widened every time he saw the factory taking shape. Every time he heard a vehicle parking in the lay-by, he'd hurry outside. Peace by Chocolate's chocolatier greeted everyone with a wave and a cheerful, "Hello! How are you?"

Moses Coady would have approved. How often had the tough priest told people they were poor enough to want it and smart enough to get it? How often had he convinced ordinary people that even the wealthiest company could trace its origins to "a one-room shack with a few rude shelves?"

The new factory officially opened on August 10, 2016. The Hadhads hoped a few people would drop by. Instead, dozens of locals milled about the yard. Standing on the front porch, Tareq tried to put his gratitude into words.

"Work is life," he said. "Whenever you go out, whenever you work, you will have interactions with your new community, and you will develop your ideas and skills." His family wanted to give back to the community that had given them so much. "This is a small community, a small town, but people here have so many big hearts. We feel that our duty now is to start this process of giving back, to pay back the community here—start hiring, offering jobs," he said. They had started a Facebook page so customers could reach them directly, and they were building a website.

Frank found Isam as the event wound down. Isam pointed solemnly at himself and then at Frank.

"Brothers," he said. "We're brothers together now." Frank agreed. He felt like they had both reached the far side of the dark woods and emerged into sunlight.

❖

It was time to progress from the plain boxes and plastic tubs they'd been using for packaging, and Neil Stephen convinced Tareq to hire a professional to take some high-quality photographs of their chocolates for the new boxes they were designing. Neil's team assembled a cutting board, nuts, coconut powder, and an assortment of chocolates.

Christian Allaire, a designer with the company, had been studying Syrian art for several months. He had noticed how tiles featured both in artwork and in everyday Syrian life and had designed a diamond of three red tiles and one blue flower separating "Peace" from "by Chocolate." He added "Est. 1986" in homage to the original business, and "a Syrian family tradition" in a nod to Tareq's original idea for the company name. Christian had also come up with what would prove to be the company's unofficial motto: "One peace won't hurt."

As the photo shoot was underway, Tareq's phone began blowing up with email alerts. Dozens of people sent him the same impossible story: Prime Minister Justin Trudeau was talking about Peace by Chocolate.

Trudeau had just delivered the keynote address at the UN Summit for Refugees and Migrants in New York. More than 300,000 refugees had sailed the risky journey across the Mediterranean Sea so far that year, and at least 3,211 had died or disappeared on the way. Most were fleeing Syria, Afghanistan, Iraq, Nigeria, or Eritrea. Many landed on the Greek island of Lesbos and stayed at a reception centre. Some 5,300 refugees, nearly 100 of them children who had lost their parents en route, were stuck on an island that only had space for 3,500.

Many Greek locals had volunteered long hours to help the refugees, giving them clothes and food as they staggered up the beach. Others had patrolled the coast in their own boats so they could pull people from the cold water when the smugglers' boats foundered. Some made sandwiches and brought fresh water. One local woman made it her job to snuggle the babies as they arrived to give their parents a chance to rest. A local fisherman told CNN how he often had to abandon his nets and become a fisher of people instead. Others offered the desperate refugees rides from the beach to the settlement centre. There was talk of awarding the island the Nobel Peace Prize.

"We are monsters if we don't do this," a resident told CNN. "Why should we be given a prize for being human beings?"

The United Nations called a meeting of heads of state to talk about migrants and refugees with a goal of creating a blueprint for a better international response. Trudeau wanted to convince his peers that in the crisis lay opportunity. Instead of reeling off numbers, Trudeau said, he wanted to share a story.

"One story among many," the prime minister said. "Because we need to remember just who we're talking about." He proceeded to describe Antigonish and the "big-hearted Canadians" who came together to bring a Syrian family to Canada.

"Back home in Damascus, the Hadhads had owned a successful business, a chocolate factory," Trudeau said. "And after they arrived in Nova Scotia — after getting acclimatized, because Canadian winters are pretty much what you'd expect — they started to look for opportunities to rebuild their business, and to rebuild their lives. And step by step, with the support of their community, they did just that.

"By May, their home-based business was doing so well that they were able to donate their profits to the Canadian Red Cross to help out with relief efforts in Fort McMurray, right on the other side of the country, which had been hit hard by wildfires. The Hadhads said that they knew what it felt like to flee their homes and lose everything, and they wanted to help by giving back what they could.

"Last month, just eight months after arriving in Canada, the family realized their dream, and opened a small chocolate factory in their new hometown." Trudeau paused. "It's called Peace by Chocolate." A cheer erupted at the back of the room. Trudeau smiled. "And you can follow them on Facebook," he concluded.

Tareq simply stared at his phone. The name of his family's business had been spoken by the prime minister at the United Nations. It was astounding. He started laughing and shaking. His phone buzzed in his hand: news outlets across Canada wanted his reaction, and hundreds of Peace by Chocolate fans posted congratulatory messages on the company Facebook page.

He took one media call, and another, and another.

"There are no words to describe the happiness that I'm feeling now that Prime Minister Justin Trudeau mentioned my family and Peace by Chocolate and the achievement we've done since we arrived here," Tareq told one reporter. "If that means anything, it means that this country has a lot of opportunities to give newcomers. We couldn't be more proud."

He told another: "Hopefully our story will inspire other countries to say that refugees can rebuild their lives and contribute to their new homes and communities."

At the photo shoot, Neil Stephen reeled in shock. He told the crew to make sure the photo was a good one. The team arranged loose nuts around two heart-shaped chocolates, one white and one brown. They added a small pyramid-shaped chocolate, a circular chocolate, and of course a maple leaf chocolate. They sprinkled the coconut dust between the food and a drawing of the Flower of Damascus, a national icon and an old Syrian symbol for peace and happiness. And then the photographer captured the image that would grace hundreds of thousands of Peace by Chocolate boxes.

With the photo done, Neil and Christian turned their attention to Peace by Chocolate's online presence. The Facebook likes ticked up swiftly, and Neil could see huge numbers of people finding the company's just-launched website.

"We need to harness this energy," Neil said. Christian agreed. They added a splash page to the site that invited people to enter their email so they'd be notified when they could place orders online. Hundreds of people signed up. Tareq's personal profile was also growing. His articulate answers in media interviews inspired invitations from groups and organizations to come and speak. He soon began booking paid gigs to address chambers of commerce, conventions, and universities. Organizers of a TEDx event at Dalhousie University in Halifax invited him to deliver a talk about his family's experiences.

All of the work Neil's team had done had been free, a gift to help them rebuild: the name, the logo, the motto, the website. Isam saw the value and told his son things needed to change.

"Tareq, we need to begin paying them," Isam said.

Neil balked at the idea. He found so much meaning in the volunteer work that he didn't want to let it go. He worried accepting Peace by Chocolate as a regular client would somehow sour the experience. He didn't want to make money from this company. He wanted to make happiness. But the Hadhads insisted, and Neil reluctantly agreed.

Everyone was starting to see what Shahnaz had long known: this could be big. Tareq laid out bold plans. He wanted to make Peace by Chocolate as big in Canada as Hadhad Chocolate had been in Syria. He dreamed of one day opening a big new factory in Antigonish. He wanted to employ many people. He pictured Peace by Chocolate as one of the top five chocolate companies in Canada. He wanted to repay Canada for the gift it had given his family, many times over.

(clockwise from above)

SAFE greets Tareq at the Halifax Stanfield International Airport in December 2015: (from left) Abdulrahim Alawashez, Vangie Babin, Sheila Sears, Lucille Harper, and Bronwen Cooke and Marc Cooke with their son, Marshall.

Tareq arrives in Halifax.

First day: Tareq learns to shovel snow.

The Red Couch Tour — "have a seat, share your story" to mark Canada's 150th birthday — made a stop to visit with the Hadhads in 2017.

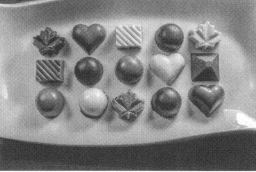

(above) Astronaut Andrew Feustel enjoys chocolate in space, 2018.

(below) Tareq with Barack Obama, 2019.

(top) Isam Hadhad, chocolatier.

(above) Batoul with Shahnaz and Isam at her high school graduation in spring 2019.

(right) The grand opening of the new factory in September 2017.

(above) Tareq and Isam meet Justin Trudeau in 2016.

(left) Tareq embraces Taghrid and Sana at his citizenship ceremony, January 2020.

Part Three

Eleven

The ruins of a once immense stone castle, built by crusaders in the thirteenth century, dominates the coastal views of Saida. It would have cost Alaa four thousand Lebanese pounds, or about $3.50, to visit the crumbling towers and battered ramparts. She knew Omar and Sana would have enjoyed visiting the Sea Castle, as it was called; they often glimpsed it on their treks through the markets and shops in Saida's old town. But Alaa had no money to spare.

For Alaa, Saida was not a historic city of beautifully restored Ottoman palaces and the striking Al-Omari Mosque, but a place of pleading hands, hungry bellies, and aching feet. She thought of Mamdouh constantly. Was he dead? Imprisoned? Would he someday try to find her? Not knowing what had happened to him seemed worse than knowing he had been killed.

Alaa measured her days in steps. How far would she have to walk to get food, water, and other essentials? How many steps could her young children take? How long would their shoes hold out? How would she get more when they did wear out? How hot would it get? Where could they sleep? Bathe? Relieve themselves? Like many displaced people, she thought about turning to a smuggler, but she could not forget what had happened to Hanan and her children.

Omar and Sana loved to look at the pictures of Uncle Tareq shovelling snow, and the landscape photos Aunt Batoul took of the strange, icy world they now called home. It seemed half mythical to their young minds. Omar loved being with his family more than anything. "I want to be with my father," he'd whimper.

Tareq had forwarded Alaa a link to Trudeau's speech at the United Nations. She called Omar and Sana over to her phone and showed them the video of Canada's prime minister telling their family's story. None of them could understand a word he said, though they did pick out "Hadhad" and "Peace by Chocolate."

Tears welled in Alaa's eyes. She told Omar and Sana that the prime minister was an important person and he was talking about them. Tareq and everyone else were working hard to bring them to Canada, she said. They had not been forgotten.

A few weeks later, as a pretty autumn settled over Nova Scotia, Alaa's phone rang. It was the Canadian embassy. The paperwork had finally been approved. She, her son, and her daughter would travel to Canada in one month. She calculated the time in Antigonish: 2 a.m. She didn't want to startle her family, so she texted Tareq the good news. He called her immediately.

"Are you talking seriously?" he whisper-shouted.

"Yes!" she assured him, laughing. He wanted to rouse his parents and tell them the good news right away. She chastised him. If he woke them from a deep sleep talking about Alaa and the children, they would think something bad had happened. Did he want to give their father a heart attack?

Tareq couldn't fall back asleep, so he kept vigil that night. He wondered if it was a coincidence that Alaa's application was approved after the prime minister shared the Hadhads' story with the world. He heard his parents stirring at 6 a.m. and knocked on their bedroom door to tell them the news. Isam, overjoyed, called Alaa right away.

"Take care of your kids until you get here," he said. "You don't need to bring anything. Just come!"

Shahnaz felt a weight shifting in her. It would really happen: she would have her daughter and grandchildren again, if they could get through the most dangerous part of their journey. Alaa hadn't yet come to the attention of soldiers or police. No one had noticed she was in the country without the proper paperwork. No one had threatened to detain her or send her back to Syria. But to get to Canada, she would have to travel to the Beirut airport and use her identification to pass through security and board the flight. All it would take was for one sour-tempered official to notice she was Syrian and pull her and her children aside. Alaa could be arrested at the airport and taken away from Omar and Sana.

Alaa had met a group of people in Lebanon who helped refugees, and they offered to travel to the airport with her. If she was detained, they would keep the children safe until she could figure out her next move.

Canadian officials told Alaa she would leave in the first week of November. When the time finally came, she packed a few suitcases with what she and her children would need. She dressed in black. The sun slipped in and out of the clouds as temperatures hit a balmy 23°C. The refugee support workers arrived. She tried to keep her breathing steady and her mood light to keep her children calm and happy. Omar and Sana were wild with excitement. All they knew was that they would see their grandmother and grandfather again soon.

Alaa moved in fear and faith. She showed her paperwork to a series of security officials, checked her luggage, and, with her children, passed through the metal detectors and suitcase scanners. No one gave her a second look. She sat at the gate, relieved but still worrying.

"Where are we going?" Sana asked again.

"Canada," Alaa told her.

Their flight was called. Alaa got her children comfortable and buckled herself into the seat. None of them had ever flown before.

The plane taxied to the runway and stopped. Alaa felt a clutch of panic. Was something wrong? Was she about to be taken off the plane? After a pause, the plane began accelerating. It lifted into the air. Omar and Sana looked at her with just a hint of fear. They all looked out the window as Lebanon receded and then disappeared under the clouds.

❖

The temperature dropped below zero outside the Halifax airport as the Hadhads paced the arrivals gate on a Monday evening in early November. The skies were clear and the mood was giddy. Isam wore a dark suit and tie with a white shirt. Tareq wore a sharp red shirt and a black suit. Shahnaz had put on a favourite blue hijab over her black coat. Batoul wore a white hijab.

Several members of CARE, the group sponsoring Alaa and her children, were at the airport. Lucille Harper and Bronwen Cooke from SAFE were also on hand to support the Hadhads. Carolyn Ray arrived and greeted the family. She'd asked Tareq for permission to film the reunion as soon as she heard that Alaa was coming at last. Although Shahnaz had initially wanted privacy for what would be a particularly intense family moment, she had reconsidered, and Tareq told Carolyn she was welcome to join them.

Batoul was excited. She held a sign reading "Peace for you in Canada." She had decorated it with stars and the Canadian flag. She told Carolyn that she had missed her older sister desperately. Shahnaz held a bouquet of flowers. Her heart raced.

The Hadhads paced around the arrivals area, glancing up at the notification screens to assure themselves that Alaa's flight was still scheduled to land. Finally, a screen showed that her plane had arrived. The Hadhads pressed against the gate separating them from the baggage carousels and looked through the doors and up the stairs. People started coming off the flight. Everyone seemed to cast a glance at the waiting party, as if hoping to be surprised by a sign with their name on it. The luggage carousel beeped and started churning out suitcases and backpacks.

Finally, someone gasped in joy. Alaa was guiding her children down the stairs and through the doors. She saw her parents. She saw Taghrid and Ahmad. Alaa adjusted her black hijab. Sana and Omar clutched her hands as they passed through the doors. Her family embraced her with tears and laughter. Alaa had been trying to cross to safety for nearly a year. Now she could reach out and grasp the hands of her family. But she knew that in doing so she was letting go of the hand of her husband, Mamdouh.

❖

The world woke up to an electoral shock on Alaa's first day in Canada: Donald Trump, the man who had pledged to ban all Muslims from entering the United States and to build walls to keep out migrants, had been elected president of the United States. Justin Trudeau called Trump a few days later to congratulate him. As it happened, Trudeau was in Nova Scotia for a series of speeches. Sean Fraser, the local MP, told the Hadhads that if they could get to Sydney, on Nova Scotia's Cape Breton Island, they might get to meet the prime minister. Isam and Tareq hopped in their car and drove for two hours to reach Sydney. They shuffled nervously in a hallway of the building where Trudeau was speaking. And then Trudeau appeared. The prime minister took off his jacket and turned to the two men. He offered Tareq a hand then pulled him in for a hug as they exchanged greetings. Trudeau turned to Isam. They embraced warmly.

"Thank you for being such an extraordinary example of the kind of strength and leadership and engagement that comes with bringing new people to Canada," Trudeau said.

"We really appreciate everything you've done for us, and for the twenty-five thousand refugees," Tareq said. Welcoming refugees, Trudeau replied, was one of the ways Canada could make a positive difference in the world.

"If you offer kindness, you will receive kindness," Tareq said, half to himself.

The three men chatted for a couple of minutes and posed for a selfie. Tareq gave the prime minister a box of chocolates to share with his family, a box Alaa had packed only four days after arriving in Canada. Then the prime minister left for his next appointment.

Tareq felt like he had been reunited with an old friend when he met Trudeau.

"Bringing refugees and showing kindness to them, it will just reflect the kindness the refugees are going to show others in the community," he said. "We really hope our message, and the prime minister, can actually talk about that with our friends at the United States and that can be a positive thing to think about."

❖

Neil called Tareq in early December to give him the good news: Peace by Chocolate could start selling online. His team had spent long hours building the website's store and setting up payment options, so people could buy chocolate from anywhere in the world. Isam had been making sure they could quickly mail the chocolates to online customers.

"I think there's going to be good demand here. Why don't we put these in bundles? People are going to want to give them as gifts," Neil told Tareq. "They could buy a five-pack."

So they offered a standard twenty-four-piece box of chocolate with a reduced price for purchases of five boxes. Neil launched the new site at the very end of the day. Christian sent out an email blast to the addresses they'd collected after the UN speech, and they prepared to leave the office. Neil's phone buzzed.

"We've sold a box of chocolates!" he told Christian.

It buzzed again. And again. And again. Peace by Chocolate was selling a box of chocolates every fifteen seconds. Orders were landing twenty at a time. Neil and Christian watched the mounting sales figure with a rising sense of dread. More than 1,500 boxes were ordered in eight hours. The Hadhads still made every chocolate, folded every box, and packed everything by hand. How could they possibly send out all of these boxes before Christmas?

He called Tareq and told him they needed to shut the website down. Tareq was taken aback, but Neil explained that the small company couldn't possibly meet its existing demands plus the mounting orders. Neil turned the sales part of the website off.

The Hadhads were going to need a bigger factory.

At the beginning of the twentieth century, a similar story had unfolded just down the road from Antigonish. John William Sobey, or J.W., was born in England in 1868, the son of a British military officer and a Pictou County woman who had met and married in Nova Scotia. They returned to Nova Scotia in 1876, and J.W. grew up with the immigrant's desire to make something of himself. His mother's family were Scottish immigrants, and she taught him their values of loyalty, self-reliance, industry, neighbourliness, social responsibility, community service, and education.

In 1907, J.W. bought a good horse and a solid cart. He drove them around Pictou County and offered farmers a deal: he'd buy their livestock right from the farm at a decent price. The farmers accepted, and J.W. then took his purchases into towns and sold them for a profit. Five years later, he opened a store in Stellarton and invited people to come to him to buy meat, fish, vegetables, animal feed, and kerosene. His business was a hit. An empire grew from those first shelves. In 1925, his son Frank, the first Sobey born in Canada, added a second store in New Glasgow and expanded to sell a full range of groceries.

By 1939, as the Antigonish Movement gathered for its first global meeting, Frank was operating six grocery stores in Nova Scotia. By 1987, the company was selling more than $1 billion of groceries each year. In 1998, it bought the Oshawa Group and took the Sobeys brand across Canada. By the time the Hadhads moved to Nova Scotia, Sobeys had annual sales of about $24.2 billion, ran 1,500 stores across Canada, and employed thousands of people. One of them was named Stephen Read.

Stephen was born and bred in Nova Scotia and grew up hearing heroic stories about his immigrant grandparents. They'd struggled to survive in Scotland. His grandfather wanted to farm, but in the 1920s a poor man like him could never buy land to get started. He heard Canada welcomed immigrants willing to work hard. He and his wife moved to Upper Dorchester, New Brunswick, and bought a large plot of land. They did well enough to sell that farm and buy a bigger one in Amherst, Nova Scotia, which is where Stephen was born. Stephen's grandparents often told him that Canada had changed their lives by giving them a chance, and that he must find the opportunity to do the same for other newcomers.

Stephen worked for Sobeys as a business manager, a job that involved identifying and meeting with potential suppliers. He first learned of Peace by Chocolate in the fall of 2016 while scrolling through Twitter, and he invited himself over to the Hadhad house.

"I'd like to bring your chocolates to Sobeys," Stephen told Tareq, Isam, and Shahnaz. "We don't currently have any local chocolate companies." He said they could start selling in the Antigonish

Sobeys and, if that went well, maybe one day expand to all of Antigonish County. They spoke for an hour or so.

Stephen returned to work and pitched his idea. Everyone at Sobeys was enthusiastic, but there was one big problem: the factory was just too small. The Hadhads could not produce enough chocolate to supply even a single Sobeys store until they moved into a larger facility that could accommodate more automation and employees. The Hadhads had told him what a monumental effort it had taken to build the shed; they didn't envision expanding again for at least a decade. Stephen wondered if Sobeys might be able to help. He decided to look into the company's real estate holdings to see if it had acquired an old store or former restaurant that it hadn't yet redeveloped.

✦

Batoul was the happiest she'd been since the Syrian war upended her life. She was still struggling with English and working late hours in an effort to make sense of biology. Every day she shook and shivered as she waited for the bus with her younger siblings. Carly and her friends had graduated from high school the previous June, and Batoul felt their absence. But Alaa was with her. Her older sister had always been her best friend, her closest confidant. To wake up every day with her in the same two-storey house, albeit an increasingly cramped one with the addition of three more family members, was a joy. To see Omar and Sana tearing around the house, mesmerized by the snow, delighted to be with their family again, warmed every moment.

The world opened like a flower in the sun. Batoul visited the Nova Scotia Community College's Port Hawkesbury campus and met other young Syrians. Batoul wasn't sure what she wanted to do with her life, but she knew that she didn't want to work in the family business. She tried driving a transport truck in the college's virtual-reality simulator and found it thrilling. Maybe she'd become a truck driver.

She also took a tour of the St. Francis Xavier University campus and could see herself studying there. She visited Antigonish's Friendship Café and practised her English with the other recent arrivals. "Life is hard," she told herself. "You should have friends."

She confessed to Alaa that she was struggling with science classes. A teacher's instruction to write in her own words threw her into a panic.

"Are they serious?" she asked her sister. "I have to create my own words?"

She plowed on, taxing her brain to translate her thoughts from Arabic to English and from English to science. The tests came every two weeks, and she struggled to pass each one.

"Please stop testing us!" she begged the teacher, only half joking.

Getting to know more Canadian teenagers revealed that they had their own struggles. In Syria, students rarely had jobs. But here, teenagers worked several days a week on top of their studies. If biology was the hardest subject, music was her best. She played Syrian pop music for her peers, and they played Canadian music for her. Batoul played the flute and loved how a sweet melody sounded the same to every ear.

Wearing modest Muslim clothes, so unremarkable in Syria, made all the Syrian women visible in a way that Syrian men were not. Batoul was very aware of how people stared at her in curiosity. People always asked her, "Where are you from?" One day she took her siblings to Dairy Queen for ice cream. As she stood in line, an older woman kept glancing at her. Finally, Batoul caught her eye.

"Hi," Batoul said.

"Hi," the woman replied, a little shyly. "Where are you from?"

"Syria."

"Oh! Are you from Peace by Chocolate?"

"We are!"

"That's so sweet. We are so lucky to have you here."

They shared a smile before ordering their ice creams.

Batoul realized she might like to work with children, so as part of a child studies course at high school, she spent a day volunteering at a daycare. Batoul read them stories and played games with them. She prepared snacks, though she didn't eat or drink herself as it was Ramadan. One confident little girl addressed Batoul as "girl" and asked her about her braces. She didn't seem to notice the hijab or modest clothing.

"This is for fixing my teeth," Batoul told her. "How's it look?"

The girl assessed her. "It looks good."

Later, when it was nap time, Batoul lay down, too. The little girl toddled over and spread a big blanket over her.

"I'm supposed to take care of you!" Batoul laughed.

Batoul grew more independent and confident as her English improved. Her friends admired her determination. "Batoul, you did really awesome today," one said to her after she'd given a presentation to her peers. "You are so strong. We can't do what you do."

Her teachers noticed her smart, steady work. "Please don't move," one whispered to her. "We need you!"

Alaa also did her best to adapt to life in small-town Canada. In Antigonish, the headscarf turned heads. When she went to apply for a driver's licence, a group of local teenage girls stared at her and giggled. Another time, a woman stopped her on the street.

"What a beautiful scarf you have on your head," she said. Alaa thanked her. She understood what the woman was really saying: I respect you; I respect your culture and your religion.

Alaa took on the responsibility of trying to bring Walaa, her husband, and their three young children to Canada. The fact that the family was living in Saudi Arabia posed a problem. They were all Syrians, but Canada rarely accepts refugees from Saudi Arabia. Alaa and her parents went to Halifax to meet with an immigration lawyer. He told them that they'd need to start by finding a private sponsor, and Alaa approached Lucille Harper. Lucille talked to other SAFE members, and they agreed to take on Walaa's case. It would take time to file the paperwork and raise the money.

"We have to fill out the application as soon as we can," Lucille told her.

Omar and Sana settled into school and quickly learned English. Omar told his mother he wanted to be a pilot; Sana wanted to be a teacher. Their Syrian accents were fading. They sounded more and more like any other Antigonish kids. One day, Alaa discovered Sana had filmed herself playing alone on the back deck.

"Boys and girls, put the garbage in the garbage can," Sana said to an unseen audience in a convincing Canadian accent. "Please, have a seat."

Alaa realized her daughter was impersonating her teacher. She laughed out loud. Her little girl was going to be just fine.

Alaa didn't bother dreaming for herself. Once, she had imagined she and Mamdouh would live their lives together, raising their children in Damascus. Her parents had imagined they would retire and live out their years in the ten-storey house. Tareq had imagined he would be a doctor. She could never have pictured herself in a small town in Canada, so why attempt to guess what would happen next? She still woke in the mornings to look out her window and wonder, *Where am I? Am I in Canada?*

But she did notice Tareq's success as a public speaker and wondered if she, too, had a story people would want to hear. A United Church women's group invited her to be their keynote speaker early that winter, and she told them about her experience as a Muslim woman in a Christian culture. In Syria and many Muslim countries, unrelated men and women never touch each other. And yet in Nova Scotia, the first thing every friendly stranger did was stick out a hand. Syrian women learned to respond to a man with his hand extended by placing their own hands on their heart and smiling. The first time Alaa tried it she braced herself, wondering if the man would respond with anger. Instead, to her surprise, he apologized, embarrassed.

Shahnaz told her she'd had a similar experience. In the fall, Peace by Chocolate won a business award in Halifax, and Isam and Shahnaz went to accept it. It was a huge honour and they hoped to make a good impression. And then the province's minister of commerce sought Shahnaz out and offered a handshake.

"I'm sorry, I can't shake your hand," she said, clutching her heart.

"No, no! I'm sorry," he said.

❖

On a frosty February 2017 morning, Tareq and Isam carefully crossed their icy driveway. Isam started the Chrysler's engine. Father and son double-checked the directions, and Isam backed out of their driveway. They followed College Street out of town. College Street became Cloverville Road. They drove for several kilometres. Finally, Isam spotted an unpromising unpaved lane forking to the right. He followed it to an ice-covered parking lot in front of a large industrial building. Stephen Read was waiting for them.

The three men penguin-walked across the slick ice toward the building. It was -15°C, and their breath formed jagged clouds. Isam thought of the Syrian sun.

Stephen explained that Big 8, a Sobeys-owned soft drink company, used a smaller building on the property. The bigger building had been empty for five years. Stephen unlocked the front door and led them inside. They walked into a narrow hallway flanked by an office and a staff room.

"Will this work for your new factory?" he asked the Hadhads.

Isam and Tareq eyed the office and chatted rapidly in Arabic. This space was perhaps 25 per cent bigger than the shed. They imagined removing the desk, sofa, and filing cabinet and filling the space with their tempering machine, fridge, and chocolate supplies. Father and son agreed it would work.

"Yes, we would love to work here," Tareq said, sweeping his hand through the office.

Stephen stared at them for a moment, trying to figure out if they were joking. "No, you will need a big building, because you will be getting international orders," he said. He opened a door at the back of the hallway and took the Hadhads into the empty space beyond.

It was huge, almost as big as Isam's first factory in Damascus's industrial district before he added more floors. Tareq and Isam took in the high ceiling and expansive floor space. Stephen walked them through the open main space and several large rooms off to the side. The entire space was theirs to rent, if they wanted it, he said, and he'd tracked down an unused walk-in fridge, which would arrive soon.

Isam's face lit up. Tareq, unusually, was lost for words. They would not have to worry about bombs, just the bears that, Stephen warned, emerged from the woods to rummage through the garbage bins in the summer.

It's way bigger than we need, Tareq thought. But his imagination filled the empty factory. He pictured his father once more commanding a team of chocolate makers, sending sweet rivers around the world to carry the Hadhads' message of peace. Standing in that empty space, Tareq stopped seeing himself as a doctor delayed. Maybe his mission wasn't just to help his father get the business going before moving on to pursue his own dreams. Maybe Peace by Chocolate was his company, too.

"Let's take it to the moon," Tareq said to his father. "There are no limits. People eat chocolate all the time. Let's get them reminded that there are people out there right now living in wars because of a lack of understanding, a lesser appreciation of life. Some people think this—Canada—is the typical kind of life all around the world. They think people come to their houses, there is warm water, there is electricity, schools for the kids. Everything is set. But this is only for twenty per cent of people on the planet; eighty per cent are struggling to find all of these things. All of this is behind the chocolate."

They heard the front door open and slam shut. A cheerful man walked in and introduced himself as the manager of the Big 8 factory. He told the Hadhads that everyone at his plant was excited about having neighbours again, especially Peace by Chocolate. A woman from Sobeys joined them. She told the Hadhads that Sobeys thought they could sell their chocolate—and not just locally, but throughout the Atlantic provinces. First, of course, they'd have to spend money to turn the empty space into a chocolate factory, and they'd have to hire workers. But it could be done.

The group parted with smiles and everyone picked their way back to their cars. Isam started the Chrysler's engine, but when he pressed down on the gas pedal the car did not move. The wheels spun on the ice. Stephen braced his feet and leaned into the back of the Chrysler, and the Hadhads learned another Canadian custom: when you see a car spinning on snow or ice, lean into the trunk and push. The Chrysler's wheels gripped the surface, and with a honk and a wave, the Hadhads sped down the unpaved lane. Isam had not yet learned to adjust his Syrian speed to local conditions.

"We are neighbours to nature," Tareq said to his father as they drove home. "We can expand in any direction we want. We have lots of space to the back and front. Imagine one hundred years of Peace by Chocolate. Where will we be?"

Once they got home, the adults gathered in the dining room. "I believe we have to take risks and expand," Tareq told them. "Maybe ten steps this time, not step-by-step. Let's get our product on the shelves. People are busy in their lives, and I want to keep our story in their minds. If we tell them we are a chocolate company, and we don't deliver them chocolate, then they couldn't taste the chocolate, and they will forget about us. But anyone that tastes our chocolate, follows us on social media, they come to us and they remember. If they taste it once, they remember our story. That's part of our mission."

After so much tumult over the last five years, it was tempting to play it safe. Grow slowly. Risk little. They had already lost everything once. And yet here they were. Yes, they could lose. But here in Canada, they would not lose peace. They decided to take the risk, placing a gigantic bet that would make them—or break them. They signed a contract with Sobeys and started planning to move Peace by Chocolate into the new space.

But Stephen soon realized he'd worked his way into another problem: if the Hadhads moved into the new facility, they'd be able to make more chocolate than Sobeys' Atlantic Canada stores could sell. He pointed this out to his boss.

His boss looked at him with the hint of a smile. "I have friends across the country," he answered. Canadians in communities across the country had welcomed Syrians and learned of the Peace by Chocolate story through the media. Stephen's boss had a hunch that they, too, would buy the chocolate if they found it on the shelves of their local grocery store.

The Hadhads scrubbed the factory clean and ordered and installed new machinery. Frank Gallant came on board as an official business adviser and took a small office. Neil Stephen, their marketing guru, somehow got roped into overseeing the food safety side of things and put in long hours ensuring everything was top grade.

It was a magical time. Isam rose early, went to the shed, played Syrian music on his phone, and made chocolate. When he closed the door, his mind returned to his homeland. Outside, it was Canada. Inside, it was a little Syria. When customers knocked on the shed door, he opened a hatch to smile, say hello, and sell them a box of chocolates.

He smiled a lot. He thought about everything and nothing. He poured his new happiness into his chocolate and found delight when that happiness reappeared as a smile on a satisfied customer's face. He knew the story would get people to buy the first box, but only the best chocolate would bring them back for a second and a third.

They added a storefront to the shed so people could come inside and browse. Drivers would spot the brown Peace by Chocolate sign from the road, park in the lay-by, and cross the street to the little shed with the red roof. They would open the white door and step inside, inhaling the scent of fresh chocolate. Wood shelves showed off the latest chocolate products and Peace by Chocolate shirts. Framed photographs of the shed's opening and other important events hung on the walls. Visitors began posing for photos on the front deck, holding the Peace by Chocolate sign in their hands, before leaving with bags full of chocolate.

The Hadhads expanded their range for the first time by creating an Easter chocolate that spring. Their first effort was a hollow egg with a lone nut rattling inside. It failed to catch on, so they switched to a solid chocolate bunny that proved popular. They planned to offer different sizes of chocolate boxes and to introduce bars and seasonal treats once the new factory was running. Shahnaz, Alaa, and Batoul worked in the chocolate shop. All through the summer, people driving through Nova Scotia stopped by the shop, said hello, took pictures, and bought chocolates. Some of them would devour the chocolates in their cars and return to buy more for the trip home. Every customer warmed the Hadhads' hearts.

People started describing Antigonish as "the home of Peace by Chocolate." The Hadhads felt profoundly honoured. The Islamic principles of kindness, peace, and sharing God's gifts were right at home in Catholic Antigonish.

Twelve

Tareq drove out to the factory in the woods every day to oversee the renovation. He awoke each morning astonished to find himself CEO of a growing chocolate company. Ten people were already working in the tiny factory at their home, and the family planned to hire twenty more when the big factory was ready to start production.

The day came on September 9, under sunny Saturday skies. They'd invited everyone they knew. Many locals had never heard of Cloverville Road, and Tareq delighted in giving them detailed directions. The factory building was blue, and outside a large white sign with gold letters read Peace by Chocolate: One Peace Won't Hurt.

On the day of the grand opening, the parking lot filled up quickly. In the crowd were many of the volunteers who had fundraised to bring the Hadhads and other Syrians to Antigonish, and who had helped them rebuild their lives. Some hoped to get a job at the new factory. With thirty employees, Peace by Chocolate would become one of the town's most important private employers, one that paid local, provincial, and federal taxes. Helping the refugees was starting to look like a sound business decision, not an act of charity. People spoke about how happy it made them to see the newcomer Syrian children playing in the parks, borrowing books at the library, and walking the streets. "It's so wonderful," one man said.

The Hadhads had made friends with a woman named Barb Stegemann, and they asked her to speak at the opening. Barb had grown up poor in rural Nova Scotia. She created a company called the 7 Virtues after her best friend, a soldier, was severely injured in Afghanistan. Barb wanted to create stability for people in turmoil through economic support. Her company sourced organic, fair-trade essential oils from places like Afghanistan, the Middle East, Rwanda, and Haiti and used them to create a line of perfumes. She'd published a successful book, *The 7 Virtues of a Philosopher Queen*, secured a venture capital deal on the TV show *Dragons' Den*, and received numerous awards in recognition of her morally infused entrepreneurship. The Hadhads asked her to speak at the factory opening—the first time a factory had opened in Antigonish in living memory.

She grabbed the microphone to cheers. "As a fellow social entrepreneur working towards peace, I am so thrilled that you came to my hometown of Antigonish!" Barb enthused. "This is the home to the Coady Institute, where we swing the doors open to the banquet for everyone to come. I'm just so thrilled that you're here." Barb went on to cite studies that showed that the Canadian provinces with the most diverse range of cultures performed the best economically. The crowd whooped and cheered. "It's because you find hope and answers and solutions in despair. You see resources where we don't see them. And now you're here to wake the rest of us up to be stronger in what we're doing."

Sean Fraser, the local MP, also spoke. He acknowledged that people worried immigrants would come to Canada and take jobs. But Nova Scotians, he said, knew that newcomers created jobs.

Standing with his family in a line beside him, Tareq looked out at the crowd. He remembered his promise to his father that six hundred people would welcome him to his new home. Here they were. When it was his turn to speak, he talked about his family fleeing the war and finding refuge in Canada. Then he spoke about the kitchen factory, the basement factory, and the tiny factory in the shed. "How marvellous is that?" he asked in genuine wonder. "Tell me, where on Earth does that happen? Is it just in Antigonish?" When his family arrived in Canada, he said, they just wanted a warm house, a warm community that opened its heart to them. "And in Antigonish, we didn't find one person. We found a whole community that has been standing with us since we came here." Yes, he said, the company's product was chocolate, but what the Hadhads were really doing was building a happier community. He thanked Sobeys and Stephen Read. One day, he said, they would ship their products of peace to the United States and around the world. Perhaps Hadhad chocolate would even be sold, once more, in Syria. "Peace is for everyone on Earth. My family is always going to fight for peace with every piece of chocolate."

He stepped down to thunderous applause. Then Isam and Shahnaz stepped up to the microphone and in broken English Isam welcomed everyone to enter the factory. He concluded with what had become his trademark phrase: "No problem!"

Volunteers offered hairnets and gloves to the long line of locals waiting to tour the factory. Tareq cut the red ribbon. Hundreds of people walked into the factory and paused to take photos of Isam. He stood, head bowed, removing chocolates from their moulds and placing them in their boxes. Dressed in his white smock, putting the finishing touches on his latest masterpieces, he looked like the artist he was.

"There's something very special about being in Antigonish," Tareq later told a reporter, looking around him. "Peace by Chocolate may not tell the general story [of refugees], but it tells what is possible. It tells other communities across the country what is possible when they all come together to support people who are fleeing war."

Peace by Chocolate passed its final inspections on October 13 and started making chocolate that same day. They created a fifteen-piece box just for Sobeys. They proudly stamped "Made in Antigonish, Nova Scotia" on every box, beside a map of the province. Pallets of chocolate were stacked onto trucks that then rumbled down Cloverville Road to carry it across Canada. Sobeys stores across the country were stocking Peace by Chocolate in special displays, usually near the checkouts, which often featured huge photos of Tareq. The stores were learning what the Hadhads had already known: it was not the chocolates but the story that first drew customers.

The company's shipping contact, worried that they were producing too much too quickly, urged them to slow down until they could see how well the chocolates sold. They flew off the shelves. Shoppers had become familiar with the Peace by Chocolate story through the news, and they were eager to support the company. It helped that the Christmas season was coming, too. People would see twenty boxes and buy them all at once. The shipping contact sent Tareq an email, this time urging him to increase production.

Neil and the marketing team came up with a dark chocolate bar mixed with cashews and designed packaging with phrases like "Kiss and Make Up," "Clean the Slate," and "Forgive and Forget" on a dark paper wrapper. Then someone had a stroke of genius: peace, they realized, is beautiful in every language. The new brightly coloured wrappers declared "*Shalom*" in Arabic, "*Paz*" in Spanish, "*Paix*" in French, and "*Wantaqo'toi*" in Mi'kmaq. A Christmas chocolate came next, followed by a foray into Valentine's Day. The holiday held a special place for the Hadhads, as that was the day Isam and Shahnaz first met in his original shop. To celebrate, Neil's team created the Unsolicited Love Advice campaign. Paper inserts in each product told the stories of ordinary Canadian couples from British Columbia to Newfoundland and what had kept them together. Many of the couples filmed videos that the company posted on its website. Brigette and Ken, a Manitoba couple married for twenty-five years, told how he, a truck driver, had met her, a waitress, and fallen in love. In the video, they wear matching teddy-bear T-shirts with their names written inside a heart on the backs. "We still kiss each other goodbye every morning when he goes to work and we still say we love each other," she says.

For Mother's Day, the family wanted to celebrate all mothers: young mothers, older mothers, grandmothers, aunt-mothers, trying-to-be mothers, grieving mothers, and gay mothers. "There is no mould for motherhood," the slogan said. They packaged seven mini chocolate bars, the wrapping on each celebrating a different type of mother. They invited people to celebrate all mothers all week.

❖

Isam woke early, thanked Allah for His blessings, and drove to the factory. He was always the first to arrive. He loved being in the parking lot at dawn, hearing the waking woods and the deep silence. No bombs. No tanks. Only birds, and the low hum of electricity.

Stepping inside the big factory as the sun peeked through the windows, he inhaled the smell of chocolate infusing every space. The sleeping machines were ready to turn the raw chocolate into Peace by Chocolate. During the busiest season, from August to May, his staff worked two shifts and made eight thousand chocolate bars every day and thousands of pieces of chocolate for the boxes. Everything in the factory was marked with two labels: one in English and the other in Arabic. The Arabic was just for him. Speaking English still felt like he was trying to talk with a frog squirming on his tongue, but an app on his phone transformed his Arabic texts into English and back again, so he often used that to communicate with his employees.

Employees tended several large tempering machines, ensuring the dark, white, and milk chocolate poured out smooth and pure. Other workers poured that chocolate into moulds divided into thirty-two individual compartments, shaping it into hearts, circles, and maple leaves. Staff placed pistachios, hazelnuts, or almonds into the warm chocolates and set them in the industrial fridge to cool. Finally, workers knocked the chocolates gently out of the moulds, placed them by hand in colour-coded paper cups, and arranged them in boxes. It was the same basic process that Isam had followed in his mother's kitchen, in the big Damascus factory, in his Antigonish kitchen, basement, and shed.

In the planning room at the back of the factory, a long piece of brown paper plotted the future: selling chocolate on Amazon, at Starbucks locations, and at Lawtons, a chain of drug stores owned by Sobeys. They'd recently spent a small fortune to buy a forklift to load the trucks, as hands alone could no longer keep pace. One day, Isam thought, they might outgrow even this factory.

Isam sat at his desk, reading contracts, inventories, and accounts, just as he had in Damascus. The difference here was that he no longer needed to also check on the latest news about the turmoil outside his factory walls. Tareq sat down in his office—the space he'd only recently imagined would house the entire operation—and looked through a list of job applications. Isam had told his son to hire people who were smarter than he was and let them work. "If you are going to tell the employee every day what to do, you are wasting your time," he explained. The Peace by Chocolate team had carefully selected the next candidates they would hire. It was the first time Tareq had personally hired people. He started typing the email: "First of all, we would like to thank you for your application to be part of the Peace by Chocolate team."

He paused, feeling an unexpected surge of emotions. He and his family had spent three long years on the run. They had turned to others to lift them up. And now, in a small way, they were able to lift up the very community that had helped them. People seemed to look at him differently on the streets. They saw him not as a refugee but as a philanthropist, and the CEO of the fastest-growing company in town.

Isam also saw his son differently. In Syria, he never expected Tareq to work in the company. But things had changed. The war had melted their old identities; Canada gave them the opportunity to mould themselves into new shapes. Isam knew how to build a successful company, and Tareq had the energy to do it. Tareq fused Syrian values with Canadian ones to create a unique brand for Peace by Chocolate. Isam was so proud of his eldest son; so proud of all his children.

Together, Isam and Tareq created a handbook for the new workers, one that emphasized the core values of Peace by Chocolate: peace, compassion, humility, integrity, reciprocity, sustainability, and customer service. They did not make chocolate, but happiness. Their employees must be happy, or the chocolate would suffer.

"No matter how rich I get, I will not be able to wear more than one pair of pants at a time. I can't sleep on more than one pillow," Isam told Tareq. "Some people think they will live forever. If you want to know where you are going, you should not forget where you come from." Isam was like Job, or Ayyub as he is called in the Qur'an. Even in the darkest days, patient Job did not complain. He was always well pleased with the Creator. "Sometimes God gives, and sometimes he takes," Job would say. Isam's expression was, "Tomorrow, tomorrow." He, too, was well pleased.

✤

One success followed another. A woman named Indira Bhatnagar Feustel, wanting to order a box of chocolates for her husband's birthday, contacted the company and spoke to Tareq. Hers was not an unusual request, except that her husband, Drew, was an astronaut and was currently orbiting the Earth in the International Space Station. The mission patch for Drew's expedition incorporated a dove carrying an olive branch in its beak as it flew above the Earth. The astronauts told reporters it represented their hope for peace and love in the world and the innate human desire to "spread our wings and explore into the future."

The company filled Indi's order for two boxes, and NASA included them in the next rocket of supplies it sent up to the station. Given that it costs upwards of $10,000 per pound to get things to space, these were likely the most expensive boxes of chocolates in human history.

When Drew received the care package and the first box of chocolates floated out, peace was very much on his mind. "We're one of the few professions that talk about humans as a species on our planet," he said in his public talks. "From space, we don't see borders on Earth. We see one world, one Earth, one fragile, frail community down on the planet. We would all do well to take better care of each other and take care of our planet." He shared the first box with the other members of the crew; he didn't tell them about the second box.

Later, when he called Indi, she told him Peace by Chocolate's story. Drew picked out an assortment of chocolate maple leaves and hearts. He pulled on his red T-shirt made by the Canadian brand Roots and swam back to the biggest window in the station. He tossed the chocolates into the air and photographed them floating around his face, the Earth visible through the window. He posted the photo online to celebrate the International Day of Peace.

"We are always looking to go beyond boundaries, we are always with the belief that even the sky is never the limit," Tareq told a reporter. "We say peace is beautiful in every language. Peace is for everyone. Now we say that peace from space is also doable."

In spring 2019, Tareq flew to Paris to speak at the Organisation for Economic Co-operation and Development, a group of thirty-four democratic governments and seventy other associate governments that sought to increase peace and prosperity. Tareq had made many trips and given many speeches. He always kept his boarding passes, and when he returned home, he taped them to his bedroom wall, a custom he started when he first came to Canada. He'd added a second, then a third. Now nearly an entire wall was filled with hundreds of boarding passes. He'd delivered more than 450 speeches around the world since 2015, travelling all across Canada and the United States, and throughout Europe.

Tareq felt a responsibility to tell his family's story so people would understand what it meant to be a refugee from war. The Canadian embassy had helped him organize the trip to Paris, including transportation to the hotel. He felt like the prime minister. He realized he was not only speaking as a Syrian but also as a new Canadian. He was proud to represent his two homelands. France, like much of Europe, had seen a rise in political parties vowing to crack down on immigration, especially from Muslim nations, and Tareq wanted to speak about the good things immigration could bring.

"When we arrived in 2016, we didn't know anyone in that community," he told a reporter. "What we did know was that Canadians were opening up their arms and welcoming my family with embracement. They were coming to them with kindness. They really offered us every single reason for us to succeed and we really wanted to give it back. That's how it happens. If you are getting kindness, you will give kindness." Immigration, he said, should not be made into a political issue. With support, many refugees would start businesses, employ people, and make their new countries better places.

There were two types of business, Tareq said: selfish and selfless. When profit comes first, the community suffers. But if the community comes first, everyone prospers. His family's company had grown to employ fifty people, and Tareq believed they'd achieve his goal of becoming one of Canada's top five chocolate producers within the next five years. In addition to providing employment, they planned to mentor ten refugees hoping to build their own successful businesses, and to help existing refugee businesses by letting them access Peace by Chocolate's distribution and retail network.

"None of us was born to hate," Tareq observed. "We learn how to hate. We learn how to be bigots. It's time to unlearn hate and bigotry."

He had a few free hours to tour the City of Lights. He visited Notre-Dame Cathedral, which had suffered a terrible fire one month earlier. He toured several chocolate shops. Parisian chocolatiers, he noticed, focused on design, each one's small, distinct shape making it easy to tell one company from another. Tareq paused on a street, wondering where to go next and feeling a little homesick for Antigonish, when a Canadian walking by did a double take and stared at his T-shirt, on which was printed the word *HOME*, with the O replaced by a map of Nova Scotia.

"Are you Tareq Hadhad?" the person asked. Tareq grinned, and the two shook hands. He was delighted to realize how much of an ambassador he was becoming, not just for Syrian refugees but for Nova Scotians and Canadians around the world.

In his speech that evening, with senior officials in Donald Trump's White House in the audience, Tareq shared his family's story and his firm belief that immigrants were an opportunity, not a problem. "Against all odds, I became the face of the new Canadian

Syrians," he said. "I believe that chocolate has been the key ingredient of my integration in Canada, and thanks to chocolate, we have been able to give back to our new community." He ended with his favourite quote: "No one can go back and start a new beginning, but everyone can start today and make a new ending."

A publisher put together a book called *My Nova Scotia Home*, featuring a range of people describing what made the land home for them, including Tareq. In fact, Tareq was such a popular speaker and had such a compelling story that the publisher asked him to speak at the book's launch.

Justin Trudeau, in Washington to meet with Nancy Pelosi, speaker of the US House of Representatives, gave Pelosi what he called "some of Canada's best chocolate, and a heart-warming Syrian refugee success story." Pelosi held up a bar of chocolate to the dozens of cameras.

"Peace by Chocolate? It sounds like an international agreement," she joked.

A few months later, Tareq waited backstage to meet former president Barack Obama, in Halifax to give a sold-out talk. Obama's words had inspired Tareq in his darkest moments, and he tossed and turned for three restless nights before the meeting, planning out what he would say. When they met, Obama grinned as widely as Tareq and gave him a warm handshake.

"Congratulations, Tareq!" the president said. "I hope all is well."

He'd been in the room when Justin Trudeau told the story of Peace by Chocolate in his UN speech, and he said he was honoured to meet Tareq. "Impossible," Tareq said to himself.

In June 2019, Batoul, now twenty, graduated from high school. Carolyn Ray was on hand to document the achievement. It had been three years since she had started following the Hadhad story for CBC. The project was meant to cover the first year, but the Hadhad story grew and grew. Most of the focus was on Tareq, Isam, and

Peace by Chocolate, but anyone with a keen eye saw Batoul always present: working in the shop, going to school, and quietly becoming a young woman determining her own future.

"I really feel happy," she told Carolyn. "I'm full of happiness today, because tonight is my graduation ceremony. I'm so excited for that. I can't describe my feelings!"

Carolyn thought about their first meeting at the airport. Batoul was too shy to say hello. That scared girl was gone, replaced by a young woman with a confident, steady gaze. She'd had to work hard to earn enough credits to graduate. The hardest part had been truly learning English as a first language.

"Sometimes there are big words in English, and I couldn't explain them. It's more stressful. That is the hardest part for me," she said. She'd attempted biology more than once before her teacher took her aside to tell her she had passed the course. Batoul was elated. And she never intended to study biology again. She hoped to study computer science. "I'd love to know how to create my own programs on the computer. That's really interesting for me." She pointed to the wall. "This is the class of 2019, for the graduates. I wrote my name here. That is really amazing."

"So now when your younger siblings come here, they will walk by your name," Carolyn said.

"Yes, they will see my name here on the wall, and I hope they are going to feel proud of me," she said. Then she laughed nervously, as if she had been caught boasting. "Hopefully."

Yvonne Quik, Batoul's English teacher for the previous two years, burst into tears when Carolyn asked her about this particular student. Wiping her eyes, she said that she'd been a teacher for thirty years, and she knew that the time she spent helping Batoul would forever stand out as a highlight of her career.

"She had a profound desire to learn, to expand herself, to integrate herself into the culture," Quik said. "You're glad for all students that they graduate, because it's a milestone in their life that propels them to another part of their life, and I'm sure as I watch Batoul walk across that stage, there'll also be great pride. But I hate to see her go."

Carolyn didn't usually get emotionally attached to the subjects of her stories, but she couldn't help taking almost a sister's pride in Batoul. She knew Batoul would continue the Hadhads' inspirational story in her own way, and Carolyn assured her readers that she would continue to share Batoul's journey.

Meanwhile, life in Lebanon was getting worse, and the situation in Syria had not improved. The members of SAFE continued their work. That July, a convoy travelled to Halifax to greet a family of seven: a father, a mother, and five children under the age of thirteen. SAFE had now brought six Syrian families to Antigonish and was working on bringing four more. It was a modern Underground Railway, and Lucille was the conductor. Other groups in the community had also sponsored refugees. Antigonish County, which recorded zero Syrians in the 2016 census, now boasted sixty-five. That represented a 2 per cent increase in the total population. Antigonish had one of the largest Syrian-Canadian communities in the province.

In October 2019, Isam's eyes were hungry for a sight he hadn't seen in seven years. In 2012, his brother Ammar had been one of the first to flee the family's ten-storey Damascus home. Ammar and his wife Kinaz took their mother, daughter Israa, and son Sami to Cairo, hoping to gather the Hadhads there. But there was no peace. More than sixty thousand people had been arrested and detained in the six years they'd sheltered in Egypt. The government executed hundreds of people. In September 2019, five hundred people were arrested during protests against government corruption.

In Damascus, Ammar had built a successful career as a women's fashion designer, starting out working for older, established companies before setting out on his own. He lost all of that in Egypt. Syrians opened semi-legal restaurants and stores, but they could lose them at a moment's notice. Ammar could not work. His children, struggled to continue their educations. When Isam and Ammar's mother died in Egyptian exile in 2017, Ammar applied to join his brother in Canada. After two years, he was finally given permission. He counted down the days. When they boarded the flight to Canada, he felt like he was, at last, going home.

At the Halifax airport, Isam pulled his Samsung from his pocket, checked the time in Saudi Arabia, and called his daughter Walaa. They hoped and prayed she and her family would soon arrive in Canada. For now, she would join the welcome via video.

Isam spotted the newcomers at the top of the stairs and waved his right hand rapidly. Ammar stretched out his arms from three feet away to close the distance. The brothers gripped right hands, then pulled in tight for a hug. They held each other for a long moment.

Ammar smiled, tired and joyful. "This is the best feeling of my life," he said. "To be reunited with my brother, my nieces and nephews. To see everyone happy. Life in Egypt was heartbreaking."

He thought he would take a month or two to settle into Canada, get his children started in school, and then turn his thoughts to his own future. They would have their own home, just down the road from Isam's family. Ammar had many working years ahead of him and he was eager to give back to start settling a debt that could never be repaid—at least, not in one generation.

Isam was proud to have helped lay the foundation for the rest to build on. Now the Hadhads had three families from the old house together again in Nova Scotia. They would rebuild their homes, one story at a time. He was as happy as he could ever remember being.

Thirteen

Tareq came up the stairs into a phalanx of photographers and a smiling group of well-wishers. This time, he didn't look behind him to see whom they waited for: he was the celebrity. It was almost exactly five years since a taxi driver first suggested that he apply to emigrate to Canada. Now, on January 15, 2020, he was the most famous of the forty-nine new Canadians about to become citizens at the Canadian Museum of Immigration at Pier 21. He had passed his citizenship test with flying colours, earning a perfect score.

He beamed at his dear friends and family at the top of the stairs: Lucille Harper, Bronwen Cooke, and Sheila Sears, who had been waiting at the airport for him on that first day; Robert and Moira Sers, who had taken him into their home; his parents and siblings; his niece and nephew; his aunt and uncle; his cousins.

"It's a really proud day for you, but it's a proud day for us, too. We're getting a fine new group of citizens," Robert told Tareq. "I grew up well aware of what good luck it is to be here. I'm just so happy for you, that you've gotten to a place where you're safe and able to prosper." Tareq embraced him, remembering the warmth of that family Christmas, the early morning breakfasts, and the sense of peace.

Tareq looked handsome in his blue suit, dark vest, and red tie, but it was his red-and-white maple leaf socks that captured the most attention. He slipped into a side room and sat down for the first of his media interviews. He wasn't introduced as a refugee or an immigrant but a "well-known entrepreneur."

"I think this country has given me an opportunity, a chance, and I'm so proud to see so many people reflecting on our story as a success for immigration in this country," he said. He thanked Canadians, and Antigonish in particular, for making it possible. He also thanked the Canadians in the military, who had sacrificed their lives to keep Canada free. "Since coming to Canada, we had one mission, a message to share with the world: it's peace," he said. "We should not take peace for granted. Peace is something we can lose in the blink of an eye. It's the noblest thing we should fight for."

MP Sean Fraser came over to offer his congratulations. Tareq posed for photographs next to a Canadian flag and in front of a window overlooking snowy Halifax Harbour and Georges Island, which centuries earlier had acted as a quarantine zone for some of the country's very first immigrants. His family stayed in the background, blending in with the families of the other new Canadians from fourteen different nations.

Just before 10 a.m., they stepped into the banquet hall that would host the immigration ceremony. Tareq took his seat in the front row and quickly started chatting to the new Canadians sitting beside him. His family and friends sat a few rows back. Soon, the hall was filled with hundreds of people. Many were there for the Hadhads, but many more were there to support the other new Canadians, people who had sacrificed just as much to call Canada home, but outside the spotlight.

A hush fell over the hall as an officer of the Royal Canadian Mounted Police led the immigration judge, premier, and other dignitaries into the room. The Mountie's boots echoed through the great hall. A child was hushed by her parents.

The judge said a few words and then led the immigrants through the oath of citizenship. Tareq's smile left his face. He closed his eyes and raised his right hand. "I swear that I will be faithful and bear true allegiance to Her Majesty Queen Elizabeth the Second, queen of Canada, her heirs and successors, and that I will faithfully observe the laws of Canada and fulfil my duties as a Canadian citizen."

The oath was repeated in French, and then cheers erupted in the hall. Tareq clapped and grinned, overwhelmed by the moment. One by one, the immigrants were invited to the front to meet the dignitaries and then sign the documents that made them full Canadian citizens. Tareq's name was called. He thought back to when the United Nations had assigned him a number, and he had refused to answer to it. Emotions overflowed in him, and he hugged each dignitary like a lost brother or sister. He signed his documents and held his certificate of citizenship in one hand and a Canadian flag in the other.

Stephen McNeil, the premier of Nova Scotia, took the microphone. Usually a dour man, the sight before him brought a broad smile to his face. For decades, young Nova Scotians had gone west for work, leaving behind an aging population that could never quite pass one million. But recent years had seen the economy improve. Some of that success was due to the many immigrants who had chosen Nova Scotia as a place to work, to raise their families, and to start new businesses. Most of the cranes building the new Halifax were bankrolled by immigrants, including many who had fled Lebanon during that nation's terrible war. McNeil was certain the new Canadians before him would help Nova Scotians create a better future.

"It's always inspiring to arrive at Pier 21, whether it's celebrating new Canadians and new Nova Scotians, whether it's celebrating Canada Day, because there's something special about this place that provides hope and optimism to whoever arrives through the doors," he said. "I cannot thank you enough for continuing to keep the Canadian dream and heritage alive."

He stopped as the new Canadians cheered. He pointed to a colleague of his in government, Rafah DiCostanzo, who had grown up in Iraq under the men-only dictatorship of Saddam Hussein and immigrated to Canada in the 1980s. She now ran a small business, worked as an Arabic translator, and had a particular interest in advocating for immigrants, women, and youth. She was elected to the legislative assembly in 2017.

The premier warned the new Canadians about the unwritten rules accompanying the oath they'd just taken. "One of them is, to be a Canadian citizen, you cannot give up your culture and heritage from where you come. In fact, it's almost your Canadian responsibility to share your history, to share your past, to share your culture with us."

He talked about 1605, the true year Canada was born, when in Port Royal in the south of today's Nova Scotia, Chief Membertou greeted the French explorer Samuel de Champlain as a son. The two groups formed the Order of Good Cheer, the oldest social order in North America. "Diversity matters and makes us all stronger," McNeil said. "Your role as a Canadian, as a Nova Scotian, is to continue to remind all of us that we have a story that's still not fully written. With each passing decade, we begin to write the new Canadian story, and you're part of it. Make sure that your heritage, your ancestors, your culture, gets written on those pages."

McNeil glanced up from his notes to look at the new Canadian citizens sitting in the front row. "Immigration is not something we should be running away from, or dividing ourselves with. It should be something we embrace, because it provides us with new hope and opportunity," he said. He smiled at Tareq. "One of them is already a successful entrepreneur, providing economic opportunities for our sons and daughters to find hopes and dreams here in our province. That's what immigration does for us."

Tareq smiled and, modest as always, looked down at his Maple Leaf socks.

The news that Tareq was a Canadian citizen made headlines from coast to coast to coast. The prime minister personally congratulated him on Twitter. Tareq told reporters the first thing he intended to do as a Canadian was to buy "a double-double with a toonie."

A few days later, he was the guest of honour at his first NHL game as the Ottawa Senators beat the Calgary Flames. The Senators gave him a souvenir jersey with the Hadhad name on it. Next he took in a Halifax Mooseheads game, collecting a second Hadhad jersey. He made an appearance on *This Hour Has 22 Minutes*, the satire show that had been the first Canadian television he'd ever watched.

Batoul, having become the first Hadhad to graduate from a Canadian high school, was approaching another milestone. She'd met a handsome man from Jordan who was living in Ontario. They were engaged with plans to marry in 2020 and start a life together in Antigonish. She still missed Syria every day. She spoke to her cousins, sisters, and friends frequently. For a long time, she had thought she might one day return to Syria to live. But now she realized she no longer wanted to. She was spending time at the Antigonish library studying for her citizenship test. As she learned about Canada's past, she realized that she was already home. Perhaps, when she became a citizen, she could return to Lebanon and Syria to visit.

Ahmad and Taghrid were doing well in school and gaining Nova Scotian accents; Ahmad was almost as tall as Tareq, and they both towered over Isam. Alaa and her children were flourishing.

The chocolate business now employed dozens of people and had ambitious plans to expand into the United States. The Hadhads still sold chocolates in the little shop next to their home.

And now Tareq was a Canadian. In the coming months, his mother, father, sisters, brother, aunt, uncle, and cousins hoped to likewise take the oath and become Canadians. They would build new lives on solid ground. One day, he was sure, Walaa and her family would join them in Antigonish. They would tell their children, and their children's children, about war, about peace, and about chocolate. And while his children would be Canadian by birth, he planned to encourage them to go online and take the citizenship test every few years, lest they forget.

Early the next morning, Tareq awoke in the pale yellow Antigonish house. He prayed and turned his mind to his new homeland. He collected his thoughts and put them into an open letter to Canada.

Dear Canada: Thank you for taking a chance on this guy who dreamed of a place to call home after losing the one he was born in. Thank you for the genuine feeling of what home looks like and how home — even in the middle of a snowy January — can be the warmest place on this entire planet. (not lying, eh!)

Home now looks amazing. Life is different when you belong. Yesterday, with pride in the heart and tears in the eyes, I officially joined the nation of peace, kindness and compassion. I proudly swore that I will faithfully observe the laws of Canada and fulfill my duties as a Canadian citizen. And the journey is just starting. O Canada!

He heard his parents waking down the hall, his sisters and brother stirring. His father would soon drive out to the factory and begin the day's work. The Hadhad house was happy. The next batch of chocolate would be sweet.

Author's Note

I sat in the Nook café on Gottingen Street eyeing my phone. No messages. I checked my coffee again. Almost gone. Should I order another? I didn't want to be jittery when he arrived. But I also didn't want an empty cup tattling that I'd arrived thirty minutes early. Was he even going to show up?

I looked out the window again. The early morning sun glared down on the glass, so I craned my neck to check the street. Cars, trucks, and buses squeezed along the old road that runs from the north to the south of Halifax. Sharply dressed architects, dishevelled homeless people, and stroller-pushing parents passed on the sidewalk.

Maybe he'd changed his mind.

I'd been watching Tareq Hadhad for almost two years. I knew the names of his mother, father, sisters, and brother. I knew of his dreams to be a doctor. I knew of his family's passion for chocolate. I knew they'd lost everything in the Syrian war and rebuilt it in Canada. But I didn't know how. How had they turned from refugees into pillars of the community so quickly?

And I didn't know how small-town Canada had truly reacted to a Middle Eastern Muslim family dropping out of the clear sky to take up residence. My previous books had documented the intense and often violent racism minorities face in Nova Scotia. Eddie Carvery was a young black man in the 1960s when Halifax bulldozed Africville, his family home for generations. He moved into the ruins in 1970 to plant his body as a living protest for justice. He was still there forty years later when I asked him if I could tell his story. And I'd written about the notorious Edward Cornwallis, the British soldier who founded Halifax and tried to exterminate the Mi'kmaq First Nation. I'd written about Daniel Paul, the Mi'kmaw elder who campaigned for decades to get the city to take down its Cornwallis statue.

Would I find the same grime under the shiny story I'd been reading about the Hadhad family and Peace by Chocolate?

I spotted Tareq half a block away, striding toward me. He walked like a man who knows his way, if not his destination. He opened the door, pulling a swirl of fallen leaves into the café. He hesitated. I leapt up and offered my hand.

"Tareq Hadhad? I'm Jon Tattrie," I said.

He shook my hand and then excused himself to order his drink. I wondered how anyone could run a chocolate factory and be so thin; I'd later learn that Tareq was often asked this, and he always joked that it was the best form of marketing.

He sat on the stool beside me. I started talking. Fast.

"I want to write a book about your family. I want to write something you can hand down to your children and grandchildren so they'll know how they came to be Canadians. I want to write a book that will take your inspiring story around the world," I said. "I want to write *Peace by Chocolate: The Book*."

He nodded and sipped his drink. He picked up the copy I'd given him of my book on Dan Paul. I told him about Dan's rise from poverty in Sipekne'katik First Nation in Nova Scotia to become one of Canada's fiercest public intellectuals; a man so powerful that when he spoke, statues fell.

"What do you think?" I asked.

"I will talk to my family," Tareq said.

We shook hands. He said he'd be in touch and stepped back into the busy street.

Actually, now that I check my notes, I see that our morning meeting was postponed and we met at noon. And I see in my calendar that we met in October 2017, which means the Cornwallis statue would not fall for another three months. According to Google Street View, there are trees on that part of the street, but maybe not near enough to create a swirl at the Nook.

And that has remained one of the biggest challenges in writing this book: how do I make factual memories seem real without slipping into fiction?

It started with the Hadhads. Once they all agreed to work with me on the book, I conducted a series of long, in-depth interviews. I drove out to Antigonish and sat with Isam, Shahnaz, and Tareq at the family table. The younger children flitted in and out of the room, shyly saying hello. I told the adults they didn't have to tell me anything, but I hoped they would tell me everything.

I recorded the interviews. Tareq translated my questions into Arabic, his parents answered mostly in Arabic, and he translated their words into English before adding his own thoughts. They had fled Syria with no photos of home, no videos, no objects they could hold and tell me about.

Tareq proved to be a skilled and compassionate translator. In fact, he only once refused to translate something for me. That was when I asked his uncle Ammar if he knew Tareq had become a celebrity in Canada. Tareq blushed and quickly moved the conversation on.

I settled into what would become my pattern for the entire book: get the story from the Hadhads and then find others who could corroborate it and enhance it with their own memories. Whenever this book tells you what people were thinking and feeling, it's because they told me what they were thinking and feeling.

After much rigamarole involving consent forms, I interviewed Natalie Jewett and Oscar Jacobs from the Canadian embassy in Beirut. I interviewed Dawn Edlund from the Department of Immigration, Refugees and Citizenship Canada to learn the inner workings of Canada's Syrian rescue operation.

I interviewed Lucille Harper and Bronwen Cooke many times about founding SAFE and supporting the Hadhads. They shared private photos, videos of events, and emails and gave me permission to quote them. I also interviewed Robert and Moira Sers.

Frank Gallant, Heather Mayhew, and Carly Mayhew-Gallant were helpful both in welcoming the Hadhads to Antigonish and in helping me write this book. I interviewed all of them, together and separately, about those early days. We met at the Hadhad house and went into the basement to spur memories about the first factory. We stood in the shed, and they told me how it came together.

I returned to the Hadhad home over and over again, slowly building relationships with each family member. They patiently answered all of my questions, even as I circled back to key moments for more details.

I interviewed journalist Carolyn Ray. She spotted the story first and told me what it was like to cover the Hadhads as they grew from a local feature to international news. I scoured the CBC archives and watched every item the broadcaster did on the family. I read all other news accounts of Peace by Chocolate that I could find.

I interviewed Jyotsna Jain, Karen Foley, and Fran Wittgens to learn the inside story of the potluck that launched Peace by Chocolate. I interviewed Neil Stephen and his team at This Is Marketing several times, and they deepened my understanding of the business. I interviewed Stephen Read about how Sobeys got involved; he's now retired, and he says that nothing in his long, successful career was as personally satisfying as his role in helping Peace by Chocolate. I interviewed Peter Wade about building the shed. I even got to interview the Canadian astronaut Drew Feustel and his wife, Indi, about how Peace by Chocolate ended up floating around the International Space Station. The section on Moses Coady draws on films, his own book, and books about him.

About halfway through the book, I realized I had a problem. I was missing big sections of the women's stories. I remembered Heather and Frank telling me how when Heather visited alone, the Hadhads would welcome her inside and offer her tea and chocolate. But when Frank visited, the women would first go upstairs to don more modest clothing. I think there was a similar barrier between us when it came to getting their stories.

I asked Shahnaz, Alaa, and Batoul if they'd be interviewed by my wife, Giselle Melanson Tattrie, who works on television documentaries. They agreed, and while Giselle spoke to them about their experiences, Tareq gave me and my young children, Roslyn and Xavier, a tour of the big chocolate factory. I supplemented those interviews with later phone conversations with Batoul and Alaa.

I went to the airport with SAFE to welcome a new family of Syrians, although they asked me not to share their names out of concern for family still in Syria. I was also there when Ammar, Kinaz, Israa, and Sami arrived in October 2019.

I shared a first draft of the book with the Hadhads. It's a big, complicated story, and many things could quite literally get lost in the translation. I wanted to be certain I was as accurate as I could be. They read through it, suggested some changes, and gave it their blessing.

The Syrian war burns into its ninth year. The government, backed by Russian air support, began 2020 attacking rebels in the north and driving two hundred thousand people out of the area. Many fled to Turkey. Turkish soldiers entered Syria to back the rebels. Since 2011, about half a million people have died. Eleven million Syrians have fled their homes.

I write this in March 2020, when COVID-19 has brought the world to almost a standstill. Every conversation begins with us acknowledging we live in unprecedented times, and yet they are times that are disturbingly familiar to people who have lived under war, who have fled as refugees, and who have seen their lives and their dreamed-of futures vanish.

I spoke to Tareq not long after Nova Scotia declared a state of emergency. He, too, is anxious. The war was tangible, he said. They could hear the explosions and see the soldiers. In contrast, he noted, "the virus is very tiny and very silent." He put things into perspective later in a social media post:

> A simple comparison: 2013: During the war that tore my immediate family apart, we were forced to LEAVE our homes, and our country. 2020: During COVID-19 crisis, we are asked to STAY in our homes with our family, and stay safe. I will take the second. Full stop.

Batoul's wedding took place this month. What would have been a Canadian Hadhad family celebration to rival anything the big Damascus house hosted was instead a small ceremony of the nearest and dearest. The photos she shared on Facebook show they found happiness, despite circumstances, which is what the Hadhads have always done.

When I started working on this book, I thought of refugees as people passing through a hard time to reach safety on new shores. But after spending so much time with the Hadhads, I've also come to see it as an amputation. They were cut out of their homeland and transplanted to mine. I've tried to imagine what it would be like if I, a Canadian, had to seek refuge in Syria. How would I break my little family's branch off the family tree? How could I lose sharing a land with my parents, aunts and uncles, dear friends, and departed ancestors? The grace with which the Hadhads, and so many other Syrians, accepted their loss and replanted themselves in new soil astonishes me.

While I have never been to Syria, learning about it for this book, and listening for hours as the Hadhads reminisced about it, brought home to me the truth of a quote I read early in my research. The French archaeologist André Parrot excavated the Mari site in Syria in the 1930s. "Everyone has two homelands," he wrote, "their own and Syria." I hope you, like me, now feel a kinship with Syria, the ancient land that birthed so much of our modern world.

Writing itself is often a loner's craft, but the best parts of this book came with the help of a trusted circle of mentors: the poet and nature writer Harry Thurston; the author and educator Wanda Taylor; the memoirist Ayelet Tsabari; the crime historian Dean Jobb; and my friend and personal favourite author (and Nova Scotia's greatest living writer), Lesley Choyce. My agent, Chris Bucci at CookeMcDermid, helped me land at Goose Lane Editions, which paired me with Jill Ainsley, the editor who turned my rough first draft into a compelling story. I tried hard to fact-check this book; I apologize if I've gotten some things wrong.

Perhaps the most important work I did on this book was to eat a lot of chocolate. In these uncertain times, I advise you to do the same. It's true: Isam is not making chocolate. He's making happiness. Take a bite.

JON TATTRIE
Halifax, Nova Scotia
March 2020

Selected Sources

While much of this book is based on original research, certain sections draw on the historical record. The following lists some of the useful works I consulted, and which the reader may explore to deepen their knowledge.

Moses Coady, *Masters of Their Own Destiny* (Harper and Brothers, 1939)

Sophie D. Coe and Michael D. Coe, *The True History of Chocolate* (Thames & Hudson, 2013)

Jim Lotz, *The Humble Giant: Moses Coady, Canada's Rural Revolutionary* (Novalis, 2005)

André Parrot, *Discovering Buried Worlds* (Philosophical Library, 1955)

Rolf Sers, M.D., *My Story of Luck* (self-published, 1990)

Allen M. Young, *The Chocolate Tree* (University Press of Florida, 2007)

His books have helped raise a church and topple a statue. He finds real stories and turns them into engines for change.

Jon Tattrie works as a journalist for CBC News in Halifax. He holds a master's degree in writing from the University of King's College. He is the author of two novels and five books of non-fiction, including *Cornwallis: The Violent Birth of Halifax, Daniel Paul: Mi'kmaw Elder,* and the bestselling biography *The Hermit of Africville.*

Tattrie's writing has been published in the *Globe and Mail, Chronicle Herald, Canadian Geographic, Saltscapes,* and *Progress Magazine,* and he has appeared on numerous radio and television programs. He followed the Hadhads' story from the day Tareq arrived and first spoke to Tareq in 2016 on the day he and his father met Prime Minister Justin Trudeau. Tattrie was captivated by Tareq's joy and hope after so much sorrow and loss. In *Peace by Chocolate,* he tells the amazing story of how the Hadhads, who lost everything in the Syrian war, rebuilt their lives in Canada—with chocolate.

Photo by Giselle Melanson Tattrie